the Quilter's
color club

Secrets of Value, Temperature & Special Effects

12 Hands-On Exercises

8 Projects

by Christine E. Barnes

C&T PUBLISHING

Text copyright © 2011 by Christine E. Barnes

Artwork copyright © 2011 by C&T Publishing, Inc.

Publisher: **Amy Marson**

Creative Director: **Gailen Runge**

Acquisitions Editor: **Susanne Woods**

Editor: **Cynthia Bix**

Technical Editors: **Teresa Stroin** and **Sandy Peterson**

Copyeditor/Proofreader: **Wordfirm Inc.**

Cover Designer: **Kristy Zacharias**

Book Designer: **Rose Sheifer-Wright**

Production Coordinator: **Jenny Leicester** and **Zinnia Heinzmann**

Production Editor: **Julia Cianci**

Illustrator: **Mary Flynn**

Photography by **Christina Carty-Francis** and **Diane Pedersen** of C&T Publishing, Inc., unless otherwise noted

Published by C&T Publishing, Inc., P.O. Box 1456, Lafayette, CA 94549

Library of Congress Cataloging-in-Publication Data

Barnes, Christine.

The quilter's color club : secrets of value, temperature & special effects : 12 hands-on exercises, 8 projects / by Christine E. Barnes.

p. cm.

ISBN 978-1-60705-009-4 (softcover)

1. Quilting. 2. Color in textile crafts. I. Title.

TT835.B269 2011

746.46--dc22

2010024417

Printed in China

10 9 8 7 6 5 4 3 2 1

Acknowledgments

I sincerely appreciate the contributions of the amazing quilters whose quilts appear in this book. Thank you for sharing your work with other quilters; you inspire them in ways you'll never know.

So many of the fabrics you see on these pages came from Sugar Pine Quilt Shop, and I'm grateful to Bonnie Bechtol and Cathy, Amy, and Sharon. It's a joy to shop and teach there. Thanks also to John Palmer of Autometrix for his precision cutting of the color wheel fabrics and accompanying mat, and to Carol Walsh, Cathy Stone, and Sharon Cook for their excellent machine quilting.

I appreciate the manufacturers who provided many fabrics for the color wheel and sample blocks: Timeless Treasures, Robert Kaufman, and Westminster Fabrics.

Many thanks to my editors, Cynthia Bix and Teresa Stroin, and to the entire C&T team for taking such good care of my book. You made the process a pleasure.

I owe my students so much—you have taught *me* how to teach color! I've learned what works because of you, and when you say "Wow!" over a mock block you've made, I share in your excitement.

To my quilting buddies, Kari Hannickel and Heidi Emmett, thank you, dear friends, for listening endlessly to my ideas, scouting quilt shows, and telling me exactly what you think.

And finally, a heartfelt thanks to my "sis" Hawton-Hill for always caring.

Dedication

In memory of my mother, Marjorie Vandewater Barnes

Contents

About The Quilter's Color Club..4–6

Let's Get Together: An Introduction to Color Concepts.......................7–17

    Value..7

    Making Mock Blocks...10

    Visual Temperature...12

    Intensity..14

    Color in Landscapes...16

Making Colors Work: A Guide to Color Combinations..........................18–29

    The Color Wheel..18

    Great Color Combinations 20

    Pattern and Texture..26

    I Love Stripes!..28

Beyond the Basics: Light Effects...30–35

    Luminosity..30

    Luster...31

    Transparency..32

    Magic Fabrics...34

    Sew Time! A Word about the Color Projects..35

Projects...36–69

    Squares and Stripes...36

    Tile Dance...40

    In & Out...44

    Galaxy...48

    Lotus Leaves Squared 52

    Luminaria...57

    Parfait Dreams...60

    Woven-Color Vest..66

Frame It!..70–71

A Quilt Show—Colorful Quilts and Wearables...................................72–93

Frequently Asked Color Questions...94–95

About the Author...96

Parfait Dreams, by Christine E. Barnes (project on page 60)

This book is for all the students who have said at the close of my workshops, "Gee, I wish we could keep doing this!" It's fun to play with fabric, of course, but what they really recognize is the value of getting together and working with color alongside other quilters. They desire an ongoing experience, a process that allows them to experiment, to succeed, and sometimes to fail, because that's the way to learn about color.

And then it dawned on me: Quilters need a casual, creative setting where they can explore color concepts one at a time and give each other feedback. Quilters need a club devoted to color!

Out of that realization grew *The Quilter's Color Club*. Here you'll:

- find a quilter-friendly approach to color, with lots of examples that bring basics like value and intensity to life.

- learn to appreciate the color wheel—it's *awesome*—and to create special effects like transparency and luminosity.

- be inspired by the color in amazing quilts made by dozens of accomplished quilters.

- apply your new knowledge with a series of twelve hands-on exercises titled Give It a Try! and with eight color projects.

 ## Working on Your Own

You can embark on this adventure with a merry band of friends or pursue color independently. As a "color club of one," your color sense will develop by leaps and bounds if you work your way through the book and apply what you learn in the exercises and projects. Follow the suggestions in Ways to Work (page 6); most apply to one person as much as to ten people. And remember, even if you're on your own, you belong to the Color Club!

Starting a Color Club

It's easy, really. All you need is a place to meet and a group of motivated, like-minded quilters. Following are a few guidelines for success.

LOGISTICS

- A small group of six to ten members is best. Any larger and you may have trouble with an abundance of enthusiasm and "crowd control."

- Plan to meet monthly to keep the ideas fresh and the momentum going. Every other week is even better—just think how much more you'll accomplish.

- Find a meeting place with good light; it makes all the difference.

- A design wall is essential, although several 32″ × 40″ foam-core boards covered in flannel are just as good. They have the advantage of being portable.

Detail of *Squares and Stripes* by Christine E. Barnes (full quilt on page 36)

Detail of *Untitled* by Naoko Anne Ito (full quilt on page 33)

WAYS TO WORK

Gather a wide variety of fabric, and if that means buying more fabric, you have my permission. I suggest at least one light, medium, and dark value (pages 7–9) of every color on the color wheel (pages 18–19). In reality, you'll want many more than 36 pieces. Quarter-yard cuts or fat quarters are plenty.

- Bring your best fabrics, not your so-so ones. This is not the time to use up your ugly fabrics.

- Look for magic fabrics (pages 34–35). They bring life to a quilt.

- Be willing to swap fabrics; you'll get so much more out of the experience if you have access to other fabrics, and your fellow Color Club members will love you for sharing.

- Strive to truly understand value, temperature, and intensity. On your own, read the text and look at the examples, then read and look again. It takes time and repetition for these concepts to sink in, but the more fluent you are in the language of color, the more fun you'll have.

- Don't rush. I suggest working with one concept, such as value or temperature, per session. You'll probably want to stretch out your study of color combinations for several meetings, and I guarantee you'll want to spend several sessions on transparency.

- Most of the color exercises consist of cut-and-paste fabric *mock blocks* (pages 10–11). Be sure to pin your completed blocks on the design wall or flannel boards for critique. You will be stunned at the beauty of your "paper quilts."

Detail of *Tile Dance* by Christine E. Barnes (project on page 40)

- Feedback is everything in the learning process. Be honest when you critique each other's work, especially when you're making mock blocks, which are so easy to change.

- When you're ready to start one of the projects, commit to making mock blocks and critiquing them before you begin your quilt. You'll be a pro at the process by then, and this is the time to get the group's input.

- Persevere! It's human nature to quit when you're almost there, but that's the time to push ahead.

Finally, I can tell you from my work as a quilter and a teacher that color is accessible to all quilters, no matter what their experience. And the best-kept color secret is this: *It's more about practice than talent.* I've seen so many quilters grow in their work, and the pleasure they get from making quilts they love is beyond measure. You can grow, too. Come on—join the Color Club!

Say the word *color*, and many quilters think first of the color wheel. But it might surprise you to learn that in this book, we start with the *characteristics* of color—value, visual temperature, and intensity—because they, as much as color itself, determine the impact of a quilt. Let's start with value, the most influential aspect of color.

 Color Cue

Hue is synonymous with *color*. In this book, the two words are used interchangeably.

Value

"Value does all of the work, and color gets all of the credit." The first time I heard that statement, I was startled and excited by its truth. In a nutshell, value is about the *lightness* or *darkness* of a color, not the color itself. An infinite number of values exist—from the lightest lights through mediums to the darkest darks—but for simplicity I think of values as light, medium, or dark.

Value performs two important functions in quilt design: It creates a sense of depth, and it makes the design read.

VALUE CREATES DEPTH

We perceive some values as closer, and others farther away. In most pieced quilts—

- light values appear to recede, and
- dark values seem to advance.

Look at the star blocks shown below. The block with dark-value star points and a light-value background appears to float against a light backdrop, giving the block a strong sense of foreground and background. But if you reverse the light and dark values—with the light fabric as the star points and the dark fabric as the background—it's as if you're looking through a cut-out star, into the distance. A sense of depth exists, but it is very different.

Placement of values—light, medium, and dark—affects depth in a traditional quilt block.

Light values don't always recede and dark values don't always come forward, of course. In appliqué, light shapes on a darker background will appear closer because they literally lie on top. An abstract or contemporary design can reverse the traditional advancing/receding aspect of value; see *Doors of Rome* (page 83).

VALUE MAKES A PATTERN READ

Now take a look at the role that value plays in establishing the design. In *Tropical Crossroads* (page 8), the dark triangles anchor the blocks, while the paler triangles shimmer in the distance. If all the triangles were medium in value, you would never see the pattern and the quilt would look flat.

Tropical Crossroads, 51½" × 55½", pieced by Christine E. Barnes, machine quilted by Teresa Leavitt, 2003.

As you gather fabrics for a quilt, ask yourself, Will these colors separate enough to read as distinct pieces, or will they merge into one? Fabric on bolts is deceiving because you're seeing large areas of color and pattern. The best way to find out is to make mock blocks (pages 10–11).

Finally, if you think only novices need to consider value, think again. Experienced quilters often determine value placement before ever thinking about which colors to use. As one quilter put it, "You can use any colors as long as the values are right."

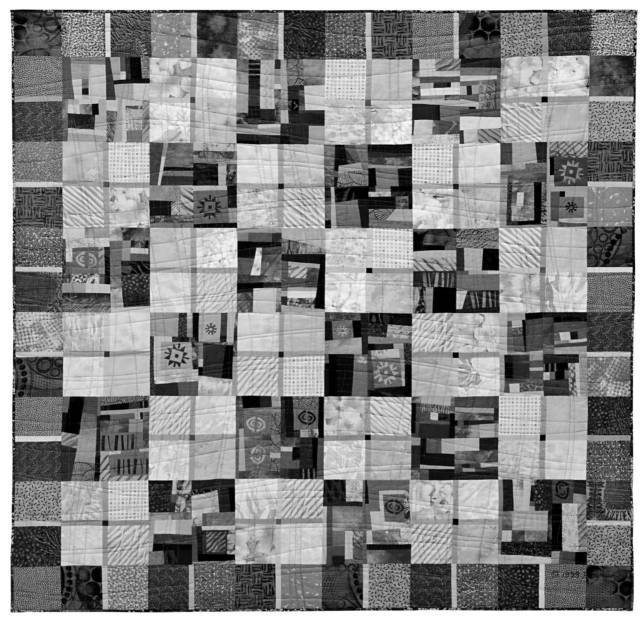

Inside Looking Out, 56″ × 56″, pieced and
machine quilted by Elaine Plogman, 1999.

Light values recede and dark values come forward in this original-block quilt. Hand-dyed,
painted, discharged, and stamped fabrics add
texture and pattern to the layers.

Give it a try!

■ Ask everyone in your Color Club to bring at least one photo of a quilt that
achieves depth through the placement of light, medium, and dark values. If
you're working on your own, look for several photos. Do the lighter values
read as background and the darker values as foreground? In quilts with mostly
medium values, what other aspects—such as pattern—help to create depth and
establish the design?

■ Disregarding color, create two simple 8″ × 8″ star mock blocks (page 7),
placing the values as shown in the background and star points. Use the same
medium-value fabric for the center square. Notice how much the sense of depth
changes when you reverse the background and the star-point values.

MAKING MOCK BLOCKS

In one of my workshops, a student was eyeing another student's sewn blocks as they went up on her design board. "I wanted mine to look like that," she said dejectedly, "not this," referring to her own blocks. A new quilter, she couldn't make the leap from her fabrics to finished blocks. If you've ever made a quilt that disappointed you—and who hasn't?—you know how discouraging the experience is. Making mock blocks can go a long way toward preventing that disappointment.

The best argument for making mock blocks is this: You simply can't predict how fabrics will look in each other's company until you cut them up and arrange them into a block. Fabrics that appear to have very different values and patterns on the bolt can blend to the point of blurring the block design; those that seem like pleasing colors as yardage may lack interest when made into a quilt. When it comes to working with color and fabric, this adage is true: You never know until you try.

A Way to Work

Following is the basic process for making and evaluating mock blocks. I recommend 9˝ blocks because they are a good, standard size and they fit easily on 11˝ × 17˝ paper.

1. Draw the block design on a sheet of 11˝ × 17˝ paper, positioning the block near the top of the sheet so you can use the lower area for notes and snips of fabric. If you're working in a group, make copies for your Color Club members (slight copy inaccuracies won't matter).

2. Analyze the block design to determine how to construct the mock block most efficiently. For the King's Crown block shown here, I cut rectangles for the background, then laid the large triangles on top of the rectangles, leaving small background triangles showing on the sides. This approach is much faster than cutting small background triangles to go on either side of the large triangles.

Speed the process by cutting and layering pieces where possible.

3. Look for ways to cut larger shapes into smaller ones. Instead of cutting four 2¼˝ squares separately for the corners in a King's Crown block, cut one 4½˝ square, then cut it in both directions to make the 4 squares.

4. Use a gluestick to adhere the cut pieces to the paper. (Hint: Put the glue on the paper, not on the back of the fabric pieces.) Go light on the glue so you can remove some pieces to audition others. You can also lay new pieces on top of the glued ones; they'll stay put long enough to see their effect.

5. Pin the completed mock blocks on your design wall or large flannel board (32″ × 40″ is ideal), stand back, and evaluate each one. If you're making a number of mock blocks on your own with a future quilt in mind, stand back at the appropriate distance. A medium-size quilt designed to hang in a living room, for example, should be viewed farther back than a small quilt meant for a hallway.

You'll quickly discover that making mock blocks is the most productive activity you can undertake, on your own or in a group. In a group setting, be willing to share fabrics and swap pieces once they're cut. And when you put your mock blocks on the design wall or board for critique, don't be afraid to say, "Take the center square off my block and try it on yours." You'll see in an instant what works and what doesn't—although be prepared for strong, differing opinions!

To create a paper quilt out of the group's blocks, pin the blocks on the design wall. It's truly a joy to see the visual impact of so many diverse blocks.

Your mock block becomes a fabric "sketch."

King's Crown Mock Block

If you'd like to try your hand at making a 9″ × 9″ King's Crown mock block, follow the cutting directions below. For your first attempt, keep it simple by choosing fabrics in these values—medium center, dark large triangles, light background, and medium-dark corners.

From the center fabric:
Cut 1 square 4½″ × 4½″.

From the large triangle fabric:
Cut 1 square 4½″ × 4½″; subcut the square twice diagonally to yield 4 quarter-square triangles.

From the background fabric:
Cut 1 strip 4½″ × 9″; subcut the strip into 4 strips 2¼″ × 4½″.

From the corner fabric:
Cut 1 square 4½″ × 4½″; subcut the square once vertically and once horizontally to yield 4 squares 2¼″ × 2¼″.

Visual Temperature

Of the three color concepts, visual temperature is the easiest for quilters to comprehend. Why? We naturally associate the warm colors—yellow, red, and orange—with the sun, heat, and fire. The cool colors—green, blue, and violet—suggest meadows, water, and sky. It's just as easy to apply this aspect of color to your quilts.

To understand the concept of visual temperature, turn to the color wheel (page 19). If you draw an imaginary line from red-violet to yellow-green, the colors on the left—yellows, oranges, and reds—are considered warm. The colors to the right of the imaginary line—greens, blues, and violets—are regarded as cool. Yellow-green and red-violet can be either warm or cool, depending on other colors in the block or quilt. Red-violet next to blue, for example, appears warm in comparison, but red-violet next to orange feels cooler.

Warm and cool colors are easy to distinguish when you look at them side by side.

Like value, temperature has an advancing/receding quality; it also sets the mood. Warm colors advance and seem lively. Cool colors recede and feel calm.

Temperature varies within a color family, too. Green is cool, but yellow-green is warmer (thanks to the greater presence of yellow), and blue-green is even cooler (thanks to the greater presence of blue). In the red family, red-orange feels warmer than red-violet.

What's the take-away lesson of visual temperature? From watching people's reactions to quilts over the years, I've concluded that the eye craves *both* warm and cool colors, with one or the other temperature predominating. All-warm quilts can be aggressive, while all-cool quilts may, well, leave you cold. The key to applying the concept of visual temperature is balance and proportion. To an all-orange quilt, add touches of cool blue-violet to bring down the temperature. To a blue-and-green quilt, introduce accents of red-orange or red. Quilts that sparkle, traditional or contemporary, almost always have a mix of warm and cool colors.

Many neutrals—black, white, gray—have a subtle visual temperature. If you're having difficulty discerning the temperature of neutrals, look at them in comparison to each other and audition them in mock blocks. A warm gray with a peach or beige cast will have a very different effect than a gray with cool, steely undertones.

What a difference visual temperature makes! The Oregon Trail block at the top almost sizzles; in the bottom block, cooler hues calm things down. Only the corner squares are the same fabric in these two blocks.

Cinnabar and Indigo, 77″ × 77″, pieced and machine quilted by Judy Mathieson, 2009.

Warm red-orange advances dramatically, while cool indigos read as background in Judy's dynamic design. Angled strips in alternating values create a visual vortex and enhance the sense of depth. Judy was inspired by an image of an ancient Roman tile floor.

Give it a try!

◼ On your own or as a group, find a photo of a mostly warm quilt, a mostly cool quilt, and one with both warm and cool colors. Which quilts appeal to you the most? In the quilt that contains both warm and cool colors, which temperature predominates?

◼ From your stash, pull five or six warm fabrics and another batch of cool ones. To the warm group add one or two of the cool fabrics, and to the cool group add one or two warm ones. Notice how each group changes with the addition of a few opposite-temperature colors.

◼ Make a King's Crown mock block (pages 10–11) in all-warm or all-cool colors. Make it again, this time using one or two fabrics of the opposite temperature. How does the block change when you balance the visual temperature?

Intensity

Value and temperature are relatively easy to grasp; intensity can be a bit more challenging. In your group sessions or on your own, spend the time it takes to master this aspect of color—your understanding will pay off in more satisfying, sophisticated quilts.

Simply put, intensity is about how brilliant or dull a color is. Synonyms for *intensity* are *saturation*, *purity*, and *clarity*. Tempera-paint colors from childhood are intense and lively. In contrast, low-intensity colors are often described as muted or dull. Some colors are decidedly intense and others are very dull, but most fall somewhere in between. Many of the fabrics shown in this book are medium in intensity.

Bright and muted versions of similar colors illustrate the power of intensity to set the mood of a fabric.

It should come as no surprise that intensity, like value and temperature, has an advancing/receding quality. Intense colors appear to be closer, while low-intensity colors seem farther away. Imagine intense circles appliquéd to a less-intense background—the circles will seem to float above the quilt.

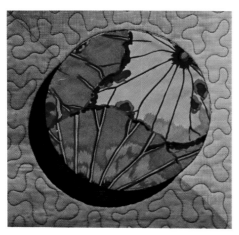

In this block from *Elegant Circles* (full quilt on page 35), the intense circle appears to float.

Following are a few tips for working with intensity:

- Although bright colors advance and dull colors recede, value can override intensity. A dull, dark blue, although cool and muted, will probably still advance because it's dark in value.

- Colors set against black appear more intense than the same colors on a white background. That's why some Amish quilts with bright colors surrounded by black look so vibrant.

- Intensity is relative: A color will look intense when placed among duller colors; the same color appears less intense among purer hues.

- Having just learned about value, you may wonder: What's the difference between value and intensity? Value has to do with the lightness or darkness of a color, while intensity has to do with its purity or dullness. As you evaluate a fabric, ask yourself: Is it light or dark? Then, is it bright or dull? You'll soon be able to tell the difference.

Color Cue

Fabric manufacturers produce lines of fabric in similar intensities because they just "go together." That's fine, but consider adding a few intense accents to your quilt. It will have more vitality, and your work will look more original.

Give it a try!

- Choose three intense fabrics and three low-intensity fabrics, and then find another three or four fabrics that fall somewhere in between. Arrange the fabrics from the most intense (brightest) to the least intense (dullest). If working in a group, let members weigh in on (and perhaps argue about) the relative intensity of the colors.

- Make two 9″ Ohio Star mock blocks, one using intense fabrics, and the other using duller ones. Stick to traditional values to make your task easier—medium center square, medium-light surrounding triangles, dark star points, and light background. If you're working as a group, arrange the intense blocks to make one paper quilt, and the low-intensity blocks to make another. Analyze the role intensity plays in the impact of each grouping of blocks.

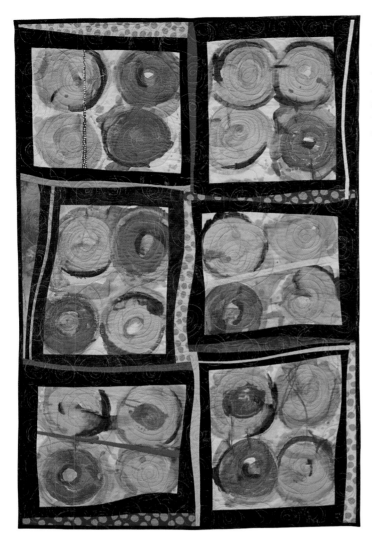
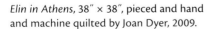

Eurythmia, 39″ × 60″, pieced and machine quilted by Rene Steinpress, 2008.

The intense colors of Rene's hand-dyed, dye-painted, and discharged fabrics appear even more vivid in the presence of black. Straight-line piecing didn't suit the organic shapes, so Rene tore the fabric and bisected the pieces with shots of bright color. The color studies of Wassily Kandinsky inspired her design.

Elin in Athens, 38″ × 38″, pieced and hand and machine quilted by Joan Dyer, 2009.

Low-intensity versions of colors similar to those in *Eurythmia* (above) are soothing. When colors are this muted, value becomes even more important in establishing the pattern. The fabrics are a mix of hand-dyes by Elin Noble and shot cottons from Greece.

COLOR IN LANDSCAPES

The natural world offers countless color cues for landscape quilts, such as the sky at sunset, a grove of trees, ocean waves; but the *characteristics* of the colors—their value, visual temperature, and intensity (pages 7–15)—are just as important. Here are some simple guidelines for realistic landscape quilts, followed by a tip for abstract compositions.

- Far-away shapes in a realistic landscape look lighter, cooler, and duller (less intense). Think of "purple mountain majesties" and what comes to mind is an image of pale, dull, violet mountains silhouetted against an equally soft sky. A distant forest is a low-intensity, nearly neutral green, while foreground foliage is brighter green.

- Foreground elements generally appear darker, warmer, and brighter (more intense). Dark values, warm hues, and intense colors advance in nature just as they do in most block quilts.

- As you go farther back in a composition, details diminish and edges become softer—it's just natural to see less detail the farther away the shapes.

- As your eye moves from the foreground through the middle ground to the background, contrasts are reduced with each plane. The farthest mountains and middle-ground hills will be closer in value than the same middle-ground hills and the foreground.

- Let the quality of the light you want to imply guide you in choosing fabrics. For a landscape on a bright day, the colors will appear clearer; on an overcast day the hues are muted. If you're trying to portray a particular time of day, keep in mind that morning light is generally softer and cooler, while afternoon light is stronger and warmer.

- There are countless naturalistic patterned fabrics designed just for quilters—grasses, sand, water, sky, to name a few—but other patterns can be just as effective, and they bring an element of originality to your design. As you did when considering value and intensity, think *depth* when you evaluate patterned fabrics: Subtle, small-scale patterns and textures used for far-away elements convey distance. For the foreground, choose larger-scale patterns.

- In an abstract landscape, of course, you can happily break any and all of the rules—*your* mountains may be bold and brilliant! But do strive for some sense of depth, even with nonrepresentational forms, to keep the design from looking one-dimensional. Notice the receding, light-value sky and darker-value foreground elements in *Earthscape* (page 87).

Give it a try!

To see how value creates depth in a simple composition, try this exercise. Quickly sketch a scene, approximately 18″ × 12″, consisting of layered mountain ranges in the background, a valley in the middle ground, and an overlook in the foreground. Don't fuss over your composition—abstract is easier than realistic. Choose these fabrics: a light fabric for the sky; medium-light and medium fabrics for the mountain ranges; a medium fabric for the valley, and a darker fabric for the foreground. As you move from foreground to background, the intensity and pattern scale (page 27) should decrease.

Celebrate the Seasons, 41″ × 31″, fused, machine appliquéd, and machine quilted by Pat Gleitsmann, 2008.

The colors change as the year unfolds in this four-part landscape, but the relative values are consistent: light sky, medium values for the distant range, and darker values for the near hills. Receding vineyards enhance the sense of depth. Pat used hand-dyed and commercial fabrics, variegated threads, acrylic paints, and watercolor crayons to depict the scene from her kitchen window.

Photo by Eric Neilsen

Marsh #17: River Bend, 44″ × 17″, fused and machine quilted by Sue Benner, 2006.

Sue establishes a strong horizon line with darker-value, less-intense trees in this abstract landscape. Brighter hues for the foreground grasses emphasize the distance between the two planes. Dye and paint on silk, cotton, and found fabrics create the colors and textures.

If you're intimidated by the color wheel—who isn't?—or if your eyes glaze over when you hear terms like *triad* and *split complement*, you're not alone in the quilting world. Quilters want to make quilts, not study color theory.

The Color Club is the place to overcome those fears. On the color wheel you'll discover magical color relationships you might never find otherwise. And if you're working as a group, you'll benefit from seeing what others do with the classic combinations. So take a deep breath—and a closer look at the color wheel.

The Color Wheel

With this invaluable tool you can build a color scheme from scratch or improve one that isn't working. The key to success with the color wheel is being able to *place* a color on it. Once you know that *cheddar* is an intense version of yellow-orange, for example, or that *merlot* is a dark-value red-violet, you can look to the color wheel to find a color or colors to go with those two. In this example, the color wheel (facing page) shows that the addition of blue-green, a color equidistant from the other two colors, makes a trio of hues known as a *triad* (page 25).

Using common names for the colors on the color wheel makes them easy to relate to. Think of the primary colors (yellow, red, and blue) and the secondary colors (green; orange; and violet, or purple) as the "plain" colors. Of course, each primary and secondary color comes in a range of values and intensities—baby blue, royal blue, and slate blue, for example.

Color Cue

I refer to green and violet as "bridging colors." Because green contains equal amounts of yellow (warm) and blue (cool), it works with every other color on the wheel. So does violet, for the same reason. If your quilt plan is lacking something, try adding one or both of these hues.

The colors that lie between the primaries and secondaries (*intermediates* in classic color theory) are appealing, versatile colors for quilters. I sometimes call them the hyphenated colors because they're easy to remember that way. Following are some common names for these colors:

- Yellow-green goes by names like lime, chartreuse, olive, avocado, and willow. It's cooler than true yellow but warmer than green.

- Blue-green is often referred to as teal, turquoise, or aqua. Thanks to the green (which is half yellow), blue-green is a bit warmer than true blue.

- Blue-violet is warmer than true blue but cooler than violet. Iris, periwinkle, and lavender blue are common names.

- Red-violet comes in a range of values and intensities. Magenta, fuchsia, and mauve (a low-intensity version) are synonyms for red-violet.

- Red-orange is sometimes difficult for quilters to identify. Think of fresh salmon and coral (light values), or terra cotta (a dark value)—oranges that have a reddish quality.

- Yellow-orange, a rich yellow with red undertones, goes by names like cheddar, mango, and papaya.

Color Cue

Quilters often ask, "Why isn't brown on the color wheel?" Browns and similar colors, like burnt umber, are usually very dark value, low-intensity versions of yellow-orange, orange, or red-orange. They would appear on a color wheel that contained a fourth ring, one with even darker-value colors.

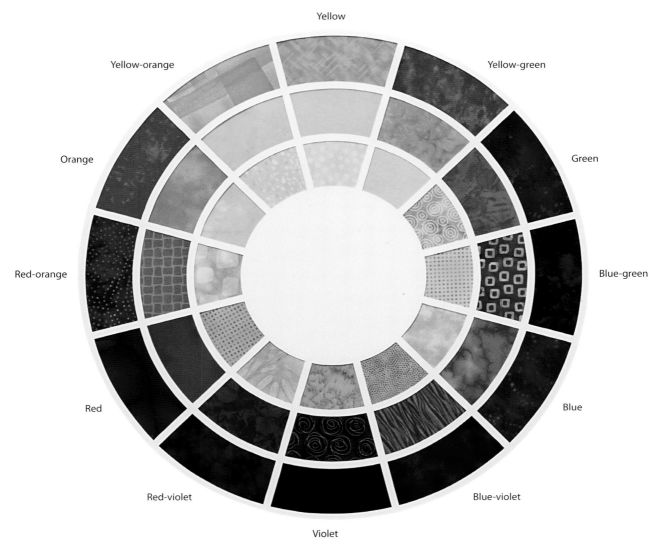

Yellow

Yellow-orange

Yellow-green

Orange

Green

Red-orange

Blue-green

Red

Blue

Red-violet

Blue-violet

Violet

My fabric color wheel contains three rings: pure hues in the middle ring, light-value versions of the colors on the inside, and dark-value versions on the outside.

Give it a try!

There is no better way to learn the color wheel than to make one! Everyone in your Color Club will take away a custom color wheel to use in planning future quilts. If you're working on your own, convince a few friends to join you for this exercise. If possible, meet in a quilt shop, where you can buy fabric to fill in any gaps.

Ask everyone to collect as many of the 12 colors on the wheel as possible, each in a light, medium, and dark value—36 in all. Have one member bring a 12″ square of foam-core board for each person, and have everyone bring glue and either rotary cutting equipment or fabric scissors.

As a group, choose and arrange the fabrics to form a color wheel, using the one shown above as a guide. Strive to maintain a similar intensity in the colors and to keep the values within each ring consistent. For example, the colors in the inner ring should have the same degree of lightness.

When you're satisfied with the result, cut good-sized swatches from the chosen fabrics and glue them to each board in concentric rings, leaving a little white space between each fabric to "pop" the colors. Don't worry about perfection—casual color wheels are more appealing. Be sure to hang your color wheel on your design wall at home. If it's accessible, you will use it.

Great Color Combinations

"I bet you would not have chosen those colors when we started this morning, but don't you love the way they look?" I say that in almost every color workshop I teach, and the answer is always, "Yes!" If you want to love the colors in your next quilt, take the time to become familiar with the color combinations. They are amazing; they are timeless. And they will open your eyes to the delicious possibilities of color-to-color relationships.

On the next pages you'll see nine color combinations. Some are loose interpretations of the classic structures, but these variations illustrate an important point: Color combinations are guidelines, not set-in-stone rules. You are free—I even encourage you—to use colors outside the classic formulas.

To illustrate the nine combinations, I've chosen either the block King's Crown or the variation Cypress, which has triangles in the corners rather than squares. I adore traditional blocks. They serve as a framework for color experimentation while honoring the history of quiltmaking.

Manic Organic, 42″ × 42″, pieced and quilted by Lynn Ticotsky, 2010.

High-energy colors form a double split complement (page 24) of red-orange, blue-green, yellow-green, and red-violet, with yellow accents.

Color Cue

Multicolored fabrics are a great way to sneak accent colors into a color-wheel combination, making it more interesting and taking it beyond the predictable.

Give it a try!

On your own or in your Color Club, make at least one mock block (pages 10–11) of each combination on the following pages. Be prepared to bend the rules and use a few unexpected colors or slight variations in the colors dictated by the classic combination. It's all right to cheat, really. Analyze which blocks work, which ones don't, and why. If you're dissatisfied, the problem probably lies with value (pages 7–9) or intensity (pages 14–15), rather than color itself.

NEUTRAL

Technically, a neutral combination consists of black, white, and any value of true gray. To these noncolors, many quilters add an accent color, such as red, for punch. I bend the definition of neutral to include "new neutrals"—very low-intensity colors such as beige, celadon, or grayed taupe. Examples abound in the natural world: rocks, bark, and faded leaves display an exquisite array of very low-intensity hues.

Whether you're going for a true neutral combination or one that includes new neutrals, strive for a good mix of pattern and texture among your fabrics (pages 26–27). The block shown here includes a variety of patterns: a naturalistic design with low-intensity red, green, and blue for the center square; a dark charcoal tone-on-tone for the large triangles; a gradated gray for the background; and an ikat stripe for the corners.

This block also illustrates the importance of value (pages 7–9) in a neutral combination. A true black—the darkest value—would make the large triangles jump out and overwhelm the other fabrics. A background of solid dark-value gray would blend with the triangles and corner squares. Here, value does much—though not all—of the work.

Neutral

MONOCHROMATIC

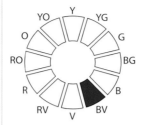

A one-color scheme relies on variations in value and intensity—on contrasts *other than* color itself. A block design that calls for more, rather than fewer, fabrics gives you the opportunity to achieve the greatest variety.

A true one-color quilt is almost impossible to create because fabrics in your chosen hue won't be exactly the same color—many different yellow-greens exist, for example. Feel free to include slightly warmer or cooler versions of your color. In a red-violet quilt, for instance, some of the fabrics may be closer to true red, with others leaning more toward violet. Just don't get too carried away, or your one-color scheme will become analogous (page 22).

When a monochromatic scheme doesn't work, the culprit is usually value. Without a mix of values, from light to medium to dark, a one-color quilt will look flat. Slight variations in intensity can give a block depth and sophistication, too; one fabric might be clear and pure, while another is more muted.

In this blue-violet example, additional colors in the center fabric act as accents, and a bold, black-and-white geometric anchors the corners.

Monochromatic

ANALOGOUS

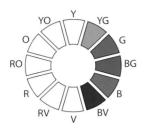

An analogous scheme consists of colors adjacent on the color wheel, such as orange, red-orange, and red. All colors must have a common hue—red in this example, because orange is half red, and red-orange is three-fourths red.

How many colors make up an analogous scheme? Any three adjacent colors on the color wheel qualify. A wider scheme consists of four colors—three colors that lie between two primaries, plus one of those primaries. Sound complicated? It's not. On the mini-wheel, look at the three colors between yellow and blue—yellow-green, green, and blue-green. Then add blue *or* yellow to make a four-color analogous combination.

I like to cheat this combination, however, with a livelier five-color scheme made up of colors that contain varying amounts of one primary and including that primary. The fabrics in the block shown here contain yellow-green, green, blue-green, and blue. But the center fabric also has just a touch of blue-violet, and that extra color makes the block richer. Each color in this far-ranging scheme has a certain percentage of blue, and blue itself is within the span of hues. Five-color analogous combinations vary more in visual temperature than do three-color schemes simply because they cover more territory on the color wheel.

Analogous

EVERY-OTHER-ANALOGOUS

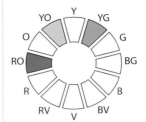

This combination is my creation, and I confess I stumbled on it by accident. Remember the hyphenated colors—yellow-green, red-orange, blue-green, and so on? They are known as the intermediates, lying between the primary and secondary colors on the color wheel. I believe quilters gravitate to these colors because each hyphenated color—yellow-green, for example—contains *unequal* quantities of two primaries. Think about it: Yellow-green is three-fourths yellow and one-fourth blue (because green is half yellow and half blue).

Any three intermediates in a row on the wheel are harmonious and are what I call an *every-other-analogous* color combination. The combination shown here—red-orange, yellow-orange, and yellow-green—contains yellow and red, obviously; but the yellow-green is ever-so-slightly cooler because it's one-fourth blue. (Remember, green is half blue.) Use the intrinsic (natural) value of each color in its pure form as a guide in choosing values. For example, pure red-orange is naturally darker in value than pure yellow-orange. In this block, I chose the corner fabrics based on those intrinsic values.

Color Cue

To an every-other-analogous scheme, add the complement of the *middle* intermediate as an accent. In the block shown here, that accent would be blue-violet, the complement of yellow-orange.

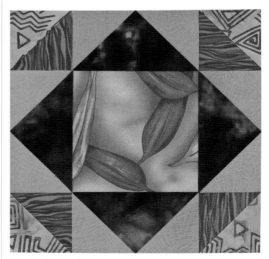

Every-other-analogous

DIRECT COMPLEMENT

Everyone knows about complementary combinations: Red and green at Christmas are traditional, and chances are you did a blue-and-orange color exercise in grade school, perhaps with construction paper. Quilters shy away from these complementary combinations of primary and secondary colors. They seem harsh; they are limiting; they look ordinary. That's a shame, because direct complements are automatically balanced in visual temperature—blue cools down orange, and yellow warms up violet. And, when you use complements in their intrinsic values—yellow is naturally lighter than violet, for example—you are more likely to achieve depth in a quilt. Let's look at some simple strategies for applying this classic color relationship to your quilts.

Any two colors opposite on the color wheel are direct complements. The combinations mentioned above are well known, but yellow-green and red-violet are complements, as are blue-violet and yellow-orange. In my experience, complements consisting of the hyphenated colors are more appealing and easier to work with because, as discussed on the facing page, each of the colors contains two primaries, but in unequal quantities.

The classic color-theory ratios of primary and secondary complements can serve as a general guide. The traditional proportions are ¼ yellow to ¾ violet; ⅔ blue to ⅓ orange; and ½ red to ½ green. You are not required to follow these formulas, of course; but with the exception of red and green, direct complements are generally most pleasing when one color predominates.

Lowering the intensity of complementary colors is the most effective way to soften the contrast. Brilliant blue-green and red-orange can overwhelm, but quieter versions of those colors, such as azure and terra cotta, are easier on the eye. You'll find another tip for working with complements in the blocks shown here: Expanding a complementary combination to include other hues makes the scheme more appealing. A red-violet and yellow-green combination above becomes more interesting with the addition of blue. The blue-green and red-orange block at right also contains various values of yellow-green, plus a light-value brown. Can you imagine these blocks without the extra colors? I can't.

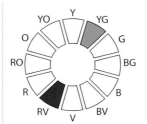

Direct complement

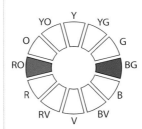

Direct complement

SPLIT COMPLEMENT

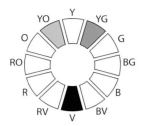

This three-color combination is probably my favorite because it's more complex than a direct complement but not as challenging as a double split (right) or a tetrad (page 25). It's also one of the most versatile, easy-to-achieve schemes, rewarding both beginners and advanced quilters with its color-and-value harmony.

As you might guess from the name, a split complement consists of one color and the colors that lie on each side of its complement. You literally *split* the complement into the two adjacent, related colors. The result is a scheme with the harmony of two nearby colors, and the visual punch of one opposing color.

Look at the color wheel (page 19) as you read about the structure of the combination shown here: It starts with violet, at the bottom of the color wheel. Violet's complement is yellow, at the top of the wheel. If you split yellow into yellow-orange on one side and yellow-green on the other, you create a beautifully balanced trio of light and dark, warm and cool colors. In this block I've used strong versions of all three colors, but it works just as well in lighter, less-intense hues like willow (yellow-green), papaya (yellow-orange), and amethyst (violet).

Split complement

DOUBLE SPLIT COMPLEMENT

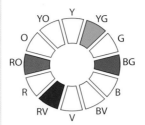

Now that you understand the structure of a split complement, you'll find a double split easy to envision. It begins with a pair of complements, such as red and green. Each one is then split into its two adjacent colors: red into red-orange and red-violet, green into yellow-green and blue-green.

Does that combo sound harsh? It's not, if you vary the values, as in the block shown here. The patterned center fabric contains all four of the colors in the scheme, and they are similar in value. But the yellow-green background is lighter than the blue-green triangles and the red-orange and red-violet corner squares. (In this block, I took advantage of a gradated blue-green fabric to create two-tone triangles.) Because the values vary, the colors coexist nicely.

Use the colors in a double split complement in different quantities. A classic color concept known as The Law of Areas suggests that you place the lighter, less intense colors in larger areas of your design and use the darker, more intense colors as accents. Yet another approach is to include different versions of each color—adding a yellow-green that is actually closer to green than yellow, for example. You'll achieve greater variety, which also softens the contrast.

Double split complement

TRIAD

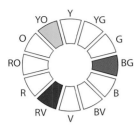

These three-color combinations are among the most pleasing of all color schemes, and they appear often in multicolored fabrics. A triad consists of three colors equally spaced on the color wheel. An easy way to find a triad is to select every fourth color on the wheel—green, violet, and orange, for example.

There are four possible triadic combinations:

- Red, yellow, and blue. Bright primaries are "kid colors," but darker, duller versions of these colors—such as goldenrod, slate blue, and brick red—are more sophisticated. Green, a bridging color (page 18), is always a nice addition to a triad of primaries; it cools and calms the warm red and yellow.

- Green, violet, and orange. If this trio sounds harsh, try varying the values or lowering the intensities. I like to add an accent of another color, such as blue-green in this combination, to broaden the appeal.

- Red-violet, blue-green, and yellow-orange; or red-orange, blue-violet, and yellow-green. I love these combinations of intermediate colors for their balance and sophistication. They are more complex than primary or secondary combinations, and the range of fabrics available in these colors is astonishing.

To avoid visual tension in any triadic scheme, make one of the colors dominant and let the remaining two play lesser roles.

Triad

TETRAD

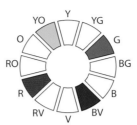

Four colors equidistant on the color wheel make up a tetrad. There are three possibilities:

- Red, green, blue-violet, and yellow-orange
- Violet, yellow, blue-green, and red-orange
- Blue, orange, red-violet, and yellow-green

The challenge with any of the tetrads is that each contains two pairs of complements, and the opposing colors may fight. The block shown below is an example of the first tetrad, and it is *very* strong. I couldn't resist the center fabric; it's such a great example of these colors, plus a very dark, dull version of red that borders on brown. When the colors are as intense as these, try spacing out the pieced blocks in a quilt with less-intense alternate blocks.

As with other complementary combinations, you can diminish the visual tension by lowering the value of all four colors. Imagine a baby quilt in soft pink, spring green, iris (light-value blue-violet), and pale papaya (light-value yellow-orange). It's both balanced and sweet.

If you look at multicolored fabrics, you'll see a surprising number of tetrads and near-tetrads. When you select one of these fabrics as a starting point, you aren't obligated to use every color present. Remember, the combinations shown on these pages are meant to inspire, not dictate, your next quilt.

Tetrad

Pattern and Texture

Moon over the Mountain; Luna, 24″ × 36″, **designed and pieced by Rebecca Rohrkaste, 2008.**

Contemporary patterns and textures in new-neutral colors (page 21) combine for a quilt that is both bold and serene; a few cool grays balance the warmer hues. Notice how value creates a sense of depth and establishes the design. The lower blocks also achieve transparency, the result of careful value placement. Inspired by a quilt by Ritsuko Shino.

PATTERN

Most of us simply choose patterned fabrics that appeal to us, and there's never anything wrong with buying what you love. But an awareness of pattern style and scale, along with a few tips for using patterned fabrics, can help you design quilts that possess both variety and unity, which is a foolproof recipe for harmony. Following are pattern styles common to quilting fabrics.

Naturalistic

Realistic elements from nature like flowers and foliage are known as naturalistic or representational patterns. Scenic elements like rocks and sky also fall into this category.

Stylized

These patterns simplify and repeat natural objects; paisley and fleur de lis are classic. With many fabrics, it's a fine line between representational and stylized patterns. Many stylized patterns are also geometric.

Geometric

Plaids, dots, and stripes combine nicely with naturalistic patterns and provide visual relief in a quilt.

Blenders

Fabrics that are semisolid, mottled, or tone-on-tone are blenders. Small-scale patterns also function as blenders.

Batik, hand-dyed, and hand-painted

"Scrunchy" color, dappled light, and painterly effects characterize these contemporary fabrics. Be sure to audition them in mock blocks; some batiks look almost neutral when cut into small pieces.

Abstract

Nonrepresentational patterns that are neither stylized nor geometric are often described as abstract.

There are other kinds of patterns—ethnic, novelty, border prints—but I tend to analyze them based on the style of the motifs. An ethnic pattern, for example, may fall into the abstract or stylized category.

The size of the motifs or design lines in a pattern is known as scale. For simplicity, pattern scale is usually described as small, medium, or large, but the range is infinite.

Funhouse, 69″ × 69″, pieced and machine quilted by Jan Soules, 2009.

Dots, dots, dots in a dizzying assortment of colors and scales are the "fun factor" in this quilt, begun in a workshop taught by Freddie Moran. Variations in pattern style and scale define the blocks; curved piecing and rickrack accentuate the shapes.

TEXTURE

Two kinds of texture are relevant to quilters: actual texture and visual texture. The actual texture of stitching and embellishment has great appeal for quiltmakers and those who love looking at (and touching) quilts. Visual texture, a kind of pattern, is the illusion of actual texture. Variation in visual texture adds interest, but too much variety can turn into chaos.

Pattern and Texture Tips

- As you gather patterned fabrics for a project, start with more, rather than fewer, pieces. It's easier to "edit" an assortment of patterns, removing those that don't work, than to add new ones to the group.

- To make the shapes in a block or quilt read as distinct pieces, choose patterns that are different in both style (floral, stripe, blender, for example) and scale (small, medium, large).

- When patterns vary dramatically, value matters less. A medium-scale stripe and a larger-scale floral, for example, will read as separate pieces in a block or a quilt, even if the values of the fabrics are similar.

- The impact of any pattern diminishes when the fabric is cut into small pieces.

- When you consider the value of a patterned fabric, look at its overall appearance, not just the background color. A fabric with a medium-value green background and black design lines will read as a medium-dark green.

Give it a try!

- On your own or in your Color Club, gather examples of each of the six pattern styles discussed on page 26, and evaluate them for scale—small, medium, or large (or somewhere in between).

- Make a King's Crown mock block (pages 10–11) using patterned fabrics that vary in style and scale. Can you distinguish the patterns in the finished block, or do they blend? Is there too much pattern? (The eye needs a place to rest.) Is there enough variation in pattern scale to make the block interesting? Work with your block (or blocks) until you find the right mix.

I Love Stripes!

At the start of my workshops, I confess that I'm hopelessly addicted to stripes; and by the end of the day, I'm always happy when my students are too. Stripes and other geometrics have a way of spacing out other patterned fabrics and visually organizing a design. And because they are typically multicolored, they automatically introduce accents of colors you might not think to include in a block or quilt.

If you're unsure about where and how to use stripes, follow the lead of interior designers. Stripes are a staple in decorating, where they act as a crisp, clean foil for naturalistic patterns and near-solid fabrics. Look through decorating magazines and you'll see that stripes bring order to a room that might otherwise look chaotic. Stripes can perform the same function in your quilts.

The stripes you'll find in quilt shops run the gamut from ultra-traditional shirting stripes to batik stripes and contemporary painterly stripes. They are either woven, with threads that are first dyed, or printed, with a right and a wrong side. An advantage to woven stripes is that triangular pieces can be flipped to make the stripes run horizontally rather than vertically, or vice versa. Batik stripes can usually be flipped, as long as the color is consistent on both sides. Although you can't flip printed stripes, they have the advantage of being much brighter than woven stripes, whose warp and weft threads blend and mute the colors.

Color Cue

If you're using a printed stripe for half-square triangles and want the stripes throughout the block to run in the same direction, cut half of the squares diagonally in one direction and the other half in the opposite direction.

Stripes are especially effective in sashing, quilt borders, and the corners of quilt blocks. If you alternate the direction of the stripes in the corners of a block like King's Crown (page 22), you'll create a lively secondary pattern where four blocks meet at the corners.

If you cut the large quarter-square triangles from one square, you can arrange them so they will appear to flow in the same direction, creating the impression that the on-point square is underneath the center square.

Other traditional blocks that lend themselves to stripes are Churn Dash, in the rectangular "bars" surrounding the center, and Jacob's Ladder, in the corners. You can center the pattern in a striped border so that it appears to connect in both directions, behind the blocks; see *Parfait Dreams*, page 60, and *Squares and Stripes*, page 36.

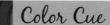 Give it a try!

Stripes can be hard to find, so it's great to work with them in the Color Club. Plan a session where you pool your striped fabrics and use one in mock blocks based on Jacob's Ladder, Churn Dash, or *Concentric Squares* (page 71). Any block that contains straight-set rectangles or squares has possibilities.

Puss in the Corner on the Courthouse Steps, 69½" × 69½", pieced by Christine E. Barnes, machine quilted by Teresa Leavitt, 2005. Inspired by Terry Atkinson's quilt *Tile Tango.*

Stripes in the background and borders of this quilt have a calming effect, a result of light-to-medium values and minimal contrast. In the blocks, darker, multicolored stripes do not dominate because the pieces are small.

Hardly Strictly Chintz, 84" × 84", pieced and machine quilted by Rebecca Rohrkaste, 2008.

Stripes in the alternate squares and the occa-sional block are a delightful contrast to the multitude of stylized and floral patterns, which Rebecca broadly refers to as "chintz." A few plaids get into the act, too; hence the name. Warm brown enhances the nuanced palette of mauve (a low-intensity red-violet), rose, and lavender, with accents of pale green and blue-green.

Photo by Sibila Savage

Have you ever looked at a quilt and said, "It just glows!" That's a special effect known as luminosity, an illusion based on light. Luster and transparency are two other light effects that captivate quilters. All three are surprisingly easy to achieve by manipulating value, visual temperature, and intensity (see pages 7–15).

Luminosity

There's a simple "recipe" for luminosity in a block or quilt: When you surround a relatively small area of *medium-value, warm, intense color* with a larger area of *darker-value, cooler, less-intense color*, the design will appear luminous, as if light and warmth are coming from behind. You can see this phenomenon at work in *Luminaria* (page 57).

Like most recipes, you can modify this one. The contrast between the glow and the surrounding area can be subtle, as long as the difference is discernible. That is, the medium,

warm, intense fabrics can be a bit *less* warm and *less* intense. (If the fabrics are too light in value, however, you'll lose the effect.) The surrounding darker, cooler, less-intense fabrics can be closer to medium in value, a little warmer, and a bit more intense. The result will be a softer glow.

Color Cue

Luminosity is relative: That is, a slightly dull, warm color will still glow against a cooler, darker color that is even duller.

Give it a try!

Choose five fabrics that are medium, warm, and intense, and eight fabrics that are darker, cooler, and duller. Cut the fabrics into 1½-inch strips and make a Log Cabin mock block, placing the warmest, most intense fabric in the center square. Use the other four medium, warm, intense fabrics for the first round of logs, followed by two rounds of the darker, cooler, duller fabrics. Trim the paper and butt the blocks against each other when you critique them to see the full effect.

Sunlight in the Forest, 63" × 54", designed, machine pieced, and machine quilted by Elaine Plogman, 2000.

Luminosity is effective even when it's confined to small accent areas. Here, shafts of light and warmth run vertically through the quilt. The background pieces are both light and dark, but they are also dull, allowing the gold and orange slivers to appear illuminated.

Luster

This light-driven illusion imparts a sense of glow, but in this case the light source comes from above or one side, rather than from behind the quilt. Sometimes, it looks like a diffuse sweep of light; in other cases it's more of a reflective glow, sometimes referred to as sheen. For an example, see *Elegant Circles* (page 35).

For a focused lustrous effect—imagine light bouncing off curled ribbon—use light values where you want to imply the first strike of light. The fabrics surrounding the lightest areas should decrease gradually in value and intensity.

To create luster across an entire quilt, make the blocks on one side or in one corner the lightest, with adjoining blocks gradually darkening in value as your eye moves to the opposite side or corner. Keep the range of values fairly narrow, avoiding very light lights and very dark darks. Luster is a tricky illusion, but when it works, your quilt will pulsate with energy and reflected light.

Give it a try!

Gather at least 10 fabrics (more if you're working on your own), in light through medium-dark values. Avoid very light or very dark fabrics. Cut three 2-inch squares from each fabric, then swap squares among your Color Club members for greater variety. Arrange and glue 25 squares, 5 across and 5 down, on a 10″ square piece of paper so the squares flow diagonally from light to dark, starting in the upper left corner. Pin the completed blocks in the same orientation on your design wall and evaluate their effect.

Coso Too, 44″ × 42″, pieced, reverse appliquéd, and hand quilted by Charlotte Patera, 1999.

Gradated fabrics make lustrous backgrounds for Charlotte's graphic quilt. The reverse appliqué figures were inspired by the rock drawings of Native Americans from the Coso Range in south central California. In the collection of the San José Museum of Quilts & Textiles.

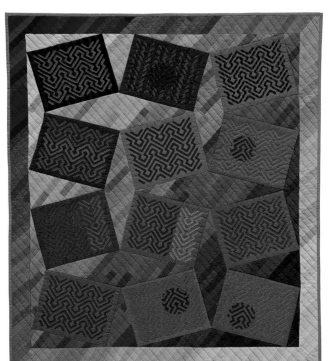

Hocus Pocus, 42″ × 52″, pieced, reverse appliquéd, and hand quilted by Charlotte Patera, 1991.

Light appears to sweep down the background from the upper left and up the border from the lower right in this dazzling quilt. Darker-value, more intense Molas dance on the surface. In the collection of the San José Museum of Quilts & Textiles.

Transparency

With transparency, we see something that makes sense, even though we know it can't be true. Think of it as trompe l'oeil—"fool the eye"—for the quilt world. Of all the light effects, this is the one that amazes, and occasionally confounds, quilters.

How does it work? Transparency assumes you can see *through* the colors. One color appears to lie on top of another, and where they overlap, a mixture of the two colors results. It's easiest to work with transparency if you consider the two source colors the *parents* and the mixed color the *child*. (Judi Warren Blaydon, an expert in creating transparencies, came up with these great terms.) The Nine-Patch blocks on the facing page illustrate simple transparencies. (See *Galaxy*, page 48, for transparencies based on an asymmetrical Nine-Patch design.)

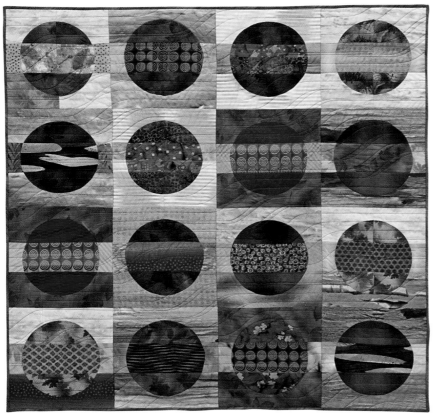

Untitled, 45" × 45", pieced by Naoko Anne Ito, machine quilted by Rebecca Rohrkaste, 2006.

Transparent bands of color flow through the circles in this ethereal quilt. Naoko made her quilt in a workshop taught by Judi Warren Blaydon, using cotton fabrics collected on her many visits to Japan.

TRANSPARENCY BASICS

A few guidelines will help you achieve convincing transparencies.

- The child fabric must be different enough from the parents to read as a separate shape.

- The child shape must be large enough to be noticed. A good rule of thumb is to make the child no less than one-fourth the size of the combined parents.

- The parent–child relationship must make sense in terms of value—a light-value parent, a dark-value parent, and a medium-value child, for example.

- The fabrics must have a similar intensity (pages 14–15) for a convincing transparency. Marked differences in intensity will destroy the illusion.

- Batiks, hand-dyes, and mottled fabrics are excellent for transparency; their variations in value, color, and pattern establish a visual flow from parent through child. (See Magic Fabrics, pages 34–35.) You can achieve the same sense of flow with many naturalistic and stylized patterns.

Create the following transparencies as 9″ Nine-Patch mock blocks. An easy way to audition fabrics is to lay a 3″ × 9″ rectangle of each parent crosswise, and then place the 3″ × 3″ child in the center, where the parents overlap. If you plan to sew these blocks, fussy cut the center squares for the strongest illusion.

Transparency of value

Transparency of value and color

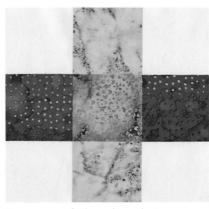

Transparency of value, color, and pattern

Value. For your first transparency, choose a light, dark, and medium value of the same color, such as the blue-violet fabrics in the block above. A medium-value fabric that lies midway between the light and dark fabrics will create the most successful transparency. Don't worry about pattern for this exercise; just focus on the values.

Value and color. Now bring color into the equation. The child should look like the logical combination of one lighter parent color and one darker parent color. In the block above, one parent is a medium yellow-green, the other is a dark blue-green, and the child contains each color, in medium-dark values.

Value, color, and pattern. In this complex transparency, the values, colors, and patterns of the parents appear in the child, as if you had poured two colors together and mixed them slightly. For the child, start with a patterned fabric that has at least two colors, and then search for the logical parent colors. Strive to find one parent with at least a hint of the child's pattern. Consider value, too—the child should lie midway between the light parent and the dark parent, as in the block above.

Color Cue

It's easy to let illogical colors creep into a transparency. If your child fabric contains violet, at least one parent must also contain violet. When evaluating fabrics for the parent and child roles, ask yourself, "Does this make sense?" It should. If you find yourself saying, "Now, where did that color come from?" keep trying. When you get it right, you'll know.

Magic Fabrics

I came up with the term *magic fabrics* when I was helping a student find the perfect fabric for a color exercise. I handed her a dappled golden-yellow piece. She cut it up, glued it to her mock-block sheet, and wow! Her block radiated light and warmth. From then on, I called it a magic fabric, and I soon began to see the potential for amazing effects in so many of my favorite fabrics.

Put simply, magic fabrics animate a quilt. Some suggest a light source coming from below the surface (luminosity) or bouncing across the surface (luster). Others imply that transparent colors overlap to create new color mixtures (transparency).

What constitutes a magic fabric? I describe many as "shot with light." They usually display variations in value—light areas among darker areas, or light-to-dark gradations—and they typically contain warm colors. (Cooler hues can convey light but rarely warmth.) Batiks, hand-dyes, and hand-painted fabrics have an organic quality, and they are among the most effective magic fabrics. Some commercial fabrics appear to be "smoldering," an illusion that lends depth and richness to even the simplest quilt.

Batiks, gradated colors, and fabrics with gentle shifts in value add vitality to a quilt.

Irregular patterns—as opposed to patterns with crisp, evenly spaced motifs—suggest movement as well. And although they are technically geometric patterns, some woven plaids look nearly iridescent. See the center of *Concentric Squares* (page 71).

Color Cue

Use magic fabrics sparingly. Side by side or throughout a quilt, they tend to fight or—worse—result in visual chaos. Give your eye a place to rest and relax.

How you use a fabric can make it magical. When background stripes run outward in a block, their lines appear to "grow" the space; see the Direct Complement block (page 23). Juxtaposing a glowing fabric with one that is duller and darker accentuates the warmth; see *Squares and Stripes* (page 36). Placing a gradated fabric in the background implies a sweep of light; see the neutral block (page 21).

Whatever their specific attributes, magic fabrics are invaluable, and it's well worth the time to seek them out and use them in your quilts. Once you see the possibilities, you'll buy fabric differently.

Give it a try!

It's easiest to spot magic fabrics when they're on the bolt. On your own or with your Color Club, visit a quilt shop and pull bolts of fabric that have "magic" potential. Compare them and decide what qualities make them magical: Are they shot with light? Gradated? Do they have organic, flowing forms or motifs? Buy your favorites and try them out in a King's Crown block or in a simple shadowed circle quilt, like the one shown on the following page.

Elegant Circles, 32" × 32", pieced by Christine E. Barnes, machine quilted by Carol Walsh, 2010.

Three very different fabrics make magic in this little shadowed circle quilt, inspired by the work of Reynola Pakusich and begun in a Judy Mathieson workshop. Light appears to bounce off the borders; triangles of the same fabrics, in other colors, glow behind the intense, patterned circles. Hand-painted fabrics in the remaining triangles and the quilt corners imply horizontal movement.

Fabrics of similar value read as distinct pieces in the blocks and border due to differences in pattern and intensity.

SEW TIME!
A WORD ABOUT THE COLOR PROJECTS

In a sense, every project that follows is a Color Club activity. You're free to make the projects on your own, of course, but you'll have even more fun if Color Club members undertake the same project and work on it in a series of get-togethers. There you can assist each other with fabric choices, evaluate your mock blocks, arrange the finished blocks "by committee," audition border fabrics, and generally help each other stay on track.

Because many of my quilts repeat the same block, but in different fabrics, I'm often asked if I still make mock blocks. I usually make four to start, but once I'm satisfied that the values are right and the intensities are sufficiently varied, I forge ahead with the real blocks. (With a wide variety of fabrics, temperature balance just happens naturally.) I suggest you do the same. Draw a finished-size block on paper, make copies, and create four mock blocks. Start the project only when you're satisfied with your plan. This is the point where it all comes together. It's time to sew!

Squares and Stripes

Designed and pieced by Christine E. Barnes, machine quilted by Sharon Cook, 2009.

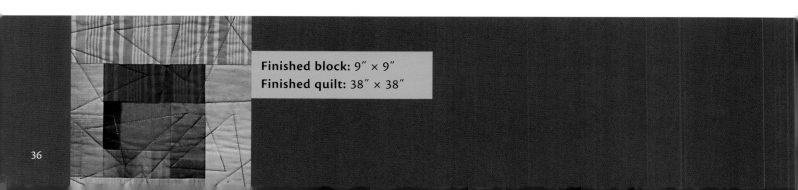

Finished block: 9″ × 9″
Finished quilt: 38″ × 38″

In planning this asymmetrical Log Cabin quilt, I gave equal consideration to the concepts of value, temperature, and intensity (pages 7–15). Wider logs of lighter-value color surround narrower, darker ones. Warm and cool colors mingle, as well as bright and dull ones. Pattern plays a role too, with painterly batiks, striated hand-dyes, subtle woven plaids, and—for visual relief—stripes. Intense center squares, a staple of traditional Log Cabin quilts, add a dash of red-hot color.

Using a striped fabric for the border and centering the stripes suggests that the design flows vertically and horizontally, beneath the blocks. This effect is more dramatic the farther you stand from the quilt.

Materials

Bright red solid or hand-dye: ¼ yard for the block centers

Darker-value fabrics: 18 different pieces, each at least 6″ × 6″, for the blocks

Lighter-value fabrics: 24 different pieces, each at least 7″ × 10″, for the blocks

Stripe: ⅞ yard for the border

Backing and facing fabric: 3⅛ yards

Batting: 46″ × 46″

CUTTING INSTRUCTIONS

From the red:

Cut 9 squares 2¾″ × 2¾″.

From the darker-value fabrics:

Cut 9 of each piece in the following sizes, varying the fabrics:

1¼″ × 2¾″ for Piece 1

1¾″ × 3½″ for Piece 2

2″ × 4″ for Piece 3

2¼″ × 5″ for Piece 4

From the lighter-value fabrics:

Cut 9 of each piece in the following sizes, varying the fabrics:

2½″ × 5¾″ for Piece 5

2″ × 7″ for Piece 6

3″ × 7¼″ for Piece 7

2¾″ × 9½″ for Piece 8

From the border fabric:

Cut 1 strip each 4½″, 5½″, 6½″, 7½″ × width of fabric for the border.

From the backing fabric:

Cut 4 strips 2½″ × width of fabric for facings.

Block Assembly

Press all seams away from the center square.

1. With right sides together and raw edges aligned, sew Piece 1 (a dark-value piece) to the lower edge of a center square. Working counterclockwise, add dark pieces 2, 3, and 4.

2. Add light-value pieces 5, 6, 7, and 8 to complete one block. Make 9 different blocks.

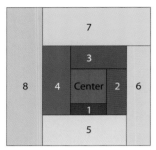

Make 9.

Quilt Construction

Refer to the quilt photo (page 36) and to the Quilt Assembly Diagram below. Follow the arrows for pressing direction.

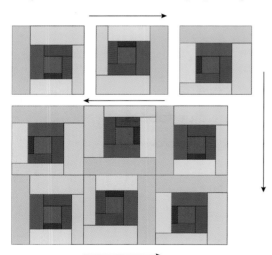

Quilt Assembly Diagram

1. Rotate and arrange the blocks as shown. Sew the blocks into 3 rows. Press.

2. Sew the rows together. Press.

3. Attach the 4½″ border to the upper edge of the quilt using a partial seam and centering the stripe pattern, if any.

Leave approximately 8″ of the strip unpinned to the quilt as shown and allow the free end to extend beyond the right edge 6″, plus a few inches.

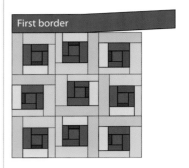

4. Stitch the partial seam. Press.

5. Add the 5½″ border to the left edge, sewing all the way to the outer edge of the first border. Press. Repeat, sewing the 7½″ border to the bottom edge and the 6½″ border to the right edge.

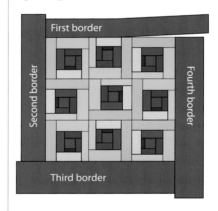

6. Return to the first border and finish stitching it to the quilt and to the fourth border. Press. Trim the excess length on each border to square up the quilt.

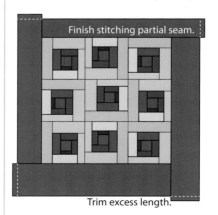

Trim excess length.

7. Layer the quilt top with batting and backing; quilt as desired. On my quilt, the blocks were quilted in a random star pattern, and the borders were quilted along every stripe.

8. To face the edges, turn under ¼" on one long edge of each facing strip and press. With right sides together and raw edges aligned, pin a facing strip to the front right and left edges of the quilt; stitch. Turn each facing entirely to the back of the quilt; none of it will show on the front. Press, and then trim the ends even with the upper and lower edges of the quilt. Slipstitch the turned-under edge of each facing to the backing.

9. Repeat for the upper and lower facings, allowing an extra ⅜" on each end to turn under before slipstitching the facing to the backing. Label your quilt.

Tile Dance

Designed and pieced by Christine E. Barnes, machine quilted by Carol Walsh, 2003.

Finished block: 8″ × 8″
Finished quilt: 50½″ × 66½″

The quilt you see here is a replica of the glass tile backsplash I designed for my kitchen, down to the colors and dimensions of the pieces. Value plays a major role: Medium-light 8˝ plain squares serve as the backdrop for darker 4˝ plain squares and multicolored 4˝ pieced squares. Temperature is an important element, too: The mix of warm and cool colors "makes the quilt dance," said a friend; hence the name. I used sueded, hand-dyed solids and tossed in a few batiks and checks to give it sparkle.

Materials

8 medium-light, cool solids: ⅜ yard each for the 8½˝ alternate squares

12 medium-dark, cool solids: ¼ yard each for the 4½˝ squares

8 other solids in a variety of values and temperatures: ⅛ yard each for the small squares, or scraps at least 8˝ × 11˝ each

Scraps of approximately 10 batiks (plus a few checks) as accents

2 yards of a warm solid for the borders and binding

1˝ rickrack: 6¼ yards for the borders

Backing fabric: 4½ yards

Batting: 59˝ × 75˝

CUTTING INSTRUCTIONS

From the medium-light, cool solids:

Cut 17 squares 8½˝ × 8½˝.

From the medium-dark, cool solids:

Cut 36 squares 4½˝ × 4½˝.

From the above 2 groups of fabrics and the 8 additional solids:

Cut at least 144 strips 1½˝ × 8˝.

From the batik and check fabrics:

Cut a variety of accent strips 1½˝ × 8˝.

From the border fabric:

Cut 2 lengthwise strips 5½˝ × 48˝.

Cut 2 lengthwise strips 5½˝ × 64˝.

Cut 4 lengthwise strips 2½˝ for binding.

Block Assembly

Follow the arrows for pressing direction.

1. Sew together the 1½˝ strips in groups of 4, striving for contrast in value and temperature and adding a batik or check strip occasionally as an accent.

2. Cut each strip set into 4 segments 1½˝ wide. Make a total of 144 segments (or more if you want a greater variety to work with).

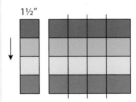

1½˝

Cut 4 segments.

3. Sew together 4 different segments, with seam allowances nesting, to make a pieced square. Press. Make 36 pieced squares.

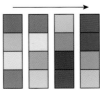

Make 36.

4. Sew 2 pieced squares and 2 medium-dark squares to make a Four Patch block as shown. Press. Make 18 blocks.

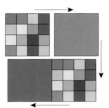

Make 18.

Quilt Construction

Refer to the quilt photo (page 40) and to the Quilt Assembly Diagram at right. Follow the arrows for pressing direction.

1. Sew 3 blocks and 2 medium-light squares into a row, orienting the blocks as shown. Press. Make 4 rows.

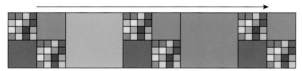

Make 4.

2. Sew 2 blocks and 3 medium-light squares into a row, orienting the blocks as shown. Press. Make 3 rows.

Make 3.

3. Join the rows. Press.

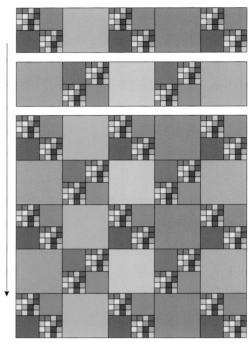

Quilt Assembly Diagram

4. Appliqué the rickrack to each border strip, placing one edge of the rickrack 2″ from one long edge of each strip.

5. Attach the first border to the upper edge of the quilt with the rickrack positioned toward the border's outer edge. Leave approximately 8″ of the strip unpinned to the quilt and allow the free end to extend beyond the right edge 5½″, plus a few inches. Stitch the partial seam. Press toward the border.

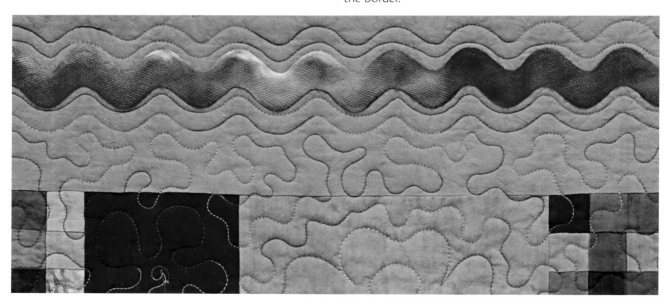

6. Add the second border to the left edge positioning the rick rack toward the outer edge, sewing all the way to the outer edge of the first border. Press toward the border. Repeat for the third and fourth borders.

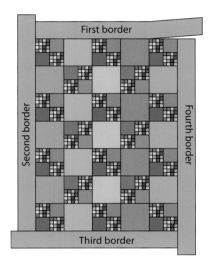

7. Return to the first border and finish stitching it to the quilt and to the fourth border. Press. Trim the excess length on each border to square up the quilt.

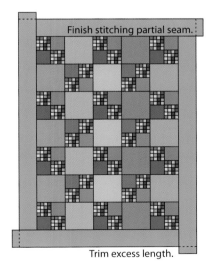

8. Layer the quilt top with batting and backing; baste. Quilt as desired. My quilt is stitched in a combination of "funky flowers" and meandering in the blocks and into the borders, with echo quilting on either side of the rickrack.

9. Join the binding strips on the diagonal; trim the seam allowances and press open. Fold the binding strip in half lengthwise, wrong sides together, and press.

10. Attach the binding using your favorite method for making mitered corners and joining the ends. Whipstitch the binding to the back of the quilt. Label your quilt.

In & Out

Designed and pieced by Christine E. Barnes, machine quilted by Carol Walsh, 2005.

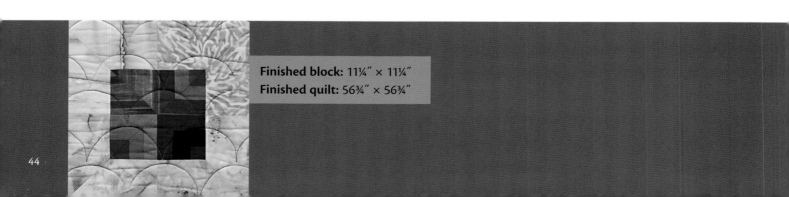

Finished block: 11¼" × 11¼"
Finished quilt: 56¾" × 56¾"

This graphic quilt relies on lots of different fabrics, but the real key is contrast in value and pattern. Variation in temperature and intensity are important too, but when you use many fabrics, you'll naturally achieve variety. The fabrics are mostly medium-to-dark stripes and lighter batiks and hand-dyes, though any two groups of fabrics that separate visually will create the in-and-out pattern. One of my favorite aspects of this quilt is what occurs at the diagonal seams, especially with batik and hand-dyed fabrics. Many of the units appear faceted, a result of the way the dappled colors converge randomly at the seams.

Materials

Medium-to-dark stripes: ¼ yard of approximately 18 fabrics*

Lighter batiks and hand-dyes: ¼ yard of approximately 18 fabrics*

Binding fabric: ⅝ yard

Backing fabric: 3¾ yards

Batting: 65″ × 65″

*You can use as few as 9 fabrics in each category, although your quilt will have less variety. If you do use only 9 each, you'll need ⅜ yard of each fabric instead of ¼ yard.

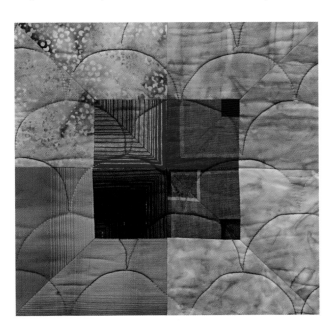

CUTTING INSTRUCTIONS

From the medium-to-dark stripes and the lighter batiks and hand-dyes:

With this cutting method, the strips will be automatically paired and perfectly aligned, ready to sew.

Pair a stripe and a batik fabric, with right sides together and selvages approximately aligned. Press to "marry" the layers. Fold the pressed fabrics over, with selvages approximately aligned, to make four layers; press again, including the center fold that's created. Cut a strip 3½″ wide through all 4 layers. If using only 9 of each type of fabric, cut a second strip.

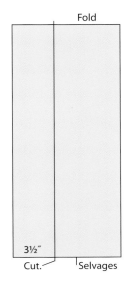

Fold

3½″
Cut. Selvages

From the binding fabric:

Cut 7 strips 2½″ × width of fabric.

MATCHING THE STRIPES

It's easy to match the stripes in the units, as shown in my quilt.

1. Pair your batik and stripe fabrics as directed in the cutting instructions, but do not fold the pressed fabrics over to make four layers. Keep only one layer of batik and stripe "married." Then cut two 3½″ strip sets *side by side*, starting from the selvages on one edge and cutting just to the center of the fabrics. Use the remaining half of the fabrics to cut two more strip sets, if desired.

2. Pin and stitch the strip sets along the inner edges as shown; press the seam allowances open. When you place the strip sets right sides together to cut the 6½″ segments shown in Step 3 (at right), you can easily match the stripe pattern. Note that there won't be a fold at one end of the strip set.

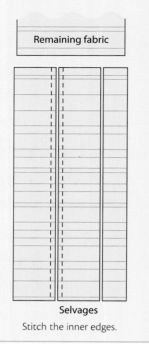

Stitch the inner edges.

Block Assembly

1. Carefully unfold the paired strip set, making sure the married pieces do not shift; stitch along one long edge. Press the seam allowances open to make one strip set. (Pressing the seam allowances open makes it easy to match them when you join the units.)

2. Fold the strip set over on itself, right sides together with the seam precisely aligned. Lift the top layer of the strip set and peek to check the alignment. Press the strip set to marry the layers, including the fold at one end.

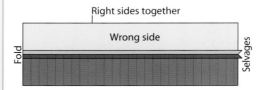

3. Trim the folded end of the strip set, then subcut the strip set into 3 segments 6½″ wide.

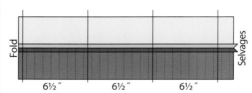

Cut.

4. Gently separate the just-cut segments to give yourself room to maneuver, making sure the layers don't shift. Cut each segment diagonally, *always cutting in the same direction.*

Cut diagonally.

5. Gently separate the sets of triangles you just cut, again making sure the layers don't shift. Pin carefully along the diagonal edges. If you aligned your strip sets accurately, you won't need to look to match the seams. Stitch, then press the seam allowances open.

Stitch.

6. You now have a total of 6 units, 3 with the stripe on the outside, and 3 with the stripe on the inside.

Make 3.   Make 3.

Tip

I leave the dog-ears on these units; they're handy when you join the units into blocks.

7. Repeat to pair the other fabrics. Make a total of 100 units: 52 with the stripe on the outside and 48 with the stripe on the inside.

8. On your design wall arrange the units to make 25 blocks, 13 with the stripe on the outside and 12 with the stripe on the inside. Strive to distribute the colors and patterns evenly across the quilt.

9. Join 4 units to make 1 block as shown. Press. Continue joining 4 units at a time to make 25 blocks.

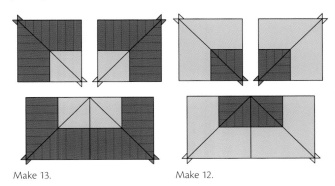

Make 13.   Make 12.

Quilt Construction

1. Join 5 blocks as shown to make the first row. Press. Make 3 rows. Join 5 blocks as shown to make the second row. Press. Make 2 rows.

Make 3.

Make 2.

2. Join the rows as shown in the Quilt Assembly Diagram below. Press.

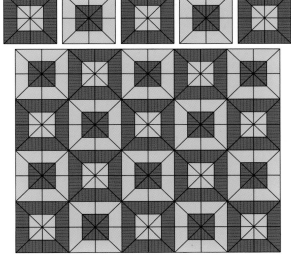

Quilt Assembly Diagram

3. Layer the quilt top with batting and backing; baste. Quilt as desired. My quilt is stitched in a clamshell pattern.

4. Join the binding strips on the diagonal; trim the seam allowances and press open. Fold the binding strip in half lengthwise, wrong sides together, and press.

5. Attach the binding using your favorite method for making mitered corners and joining the ends. Whipstitch the binding to the back of the quilt. Label your quilt.

Galaxy

Designed and pieced by Christine E. Barnes, machine quilted by Cathy Stone, 2009.

Finished block: 9″ × 9″
Finished quilt: 37½″ × 37½″

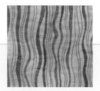

Transparency is easy to achieve using a Nine-Patch pattern—the pieces just naturally read as parents and child. (For a discussion of these terms, see Transparency, pages 32–33.) In this asymmetrical take on the traditional block, color, value, and pattern create not only the illusion of transparency but also a visual flow within each block.

Strip piece the black-and-white dot and the light parent fabrics, then cut the strip set into two segments. To make the most of the design lines in the parent and child fabrics, fussy cut the child and add the dark parent pieces to either side.

Fabric is everything when working with transparency, and you must make mock blocks (pages 10–11) to achieve the most convincing illusions. As you will discover, finding winning combinations is half the fun.

Materials

Light (vertical) parent fabric: ¼ yard for each block and the narrow inner border

Dark (horizontal) parent fabric: ¼ yard for each block and the narrow inner border

Child fabric: ¼ yard for each block and the narrow inner border*

Small-scale black-and-white dot: ⅜ yard for the blocks

Large-scale black-and-white swirl: ⅞ yard for alternate blocks and binding

Black-and-white stripe: ¾ yard for the border

Backing fabric: 2¾ yards

Batting: 46" × 46"

*Theoretically, you can use a scrap of fabric at least 5" × 4" for the center (child) of each block, but a scrap won't allow you to fussy cut the piece for the most convincing transparency.

CUTTING INSTRUCTIONS

The following instructions are for each transparency block.

From the light parent fabric:

Cut 1 piece 4½" × 9".

From the black-and-white dot:

Cut 1 strip 3½" × 9".

Cut 1 strip 2½" × 9".

From the dark parent fabric:

Cut 1 piece 3½" × 3½".

Cut 1 piece 2½" × 3½".

From the child fabric:

Cut 1 piece 4½" × 3½".

The following cutting instructions are for the remainder of the quilt.

From the parent and child fabrics:

Cut strips 1" × remaining width of fabric to total 152" for the narrow inner border.

From the large-scale black-and-white swirl:

Cut 4 squares 9½" × 9½" for the alternate blocks.

Cut 5 strips 2½" × width of fabric for the binding.

From the black-and-white stripe:

Cut 4 strips 5" × width of fabric for the borders.

Block Assembly

Follow the arrows for pressing direction.

1. Sew the black-and-white dot strips to the light parent strip. Press.

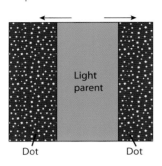

2. Subcut the strip set into a unit 2½" wide and another unit 4½" wide.

3. Sew the dark parent pieces to the child piece. Press.

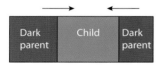

4. Join the units to make a transparency block. Press. Make a total of 5 blocks.

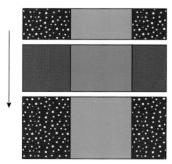

Make 5.

Quilt Construction

Refer to the quilt photo (page 48) and to the Quilt Assembly Diagram below. Follow the arrows for pressing direction.

1. Arrange the transparency blocks and the alternate blocks into a Nine Patch design. Join the blocks into rows. Press. Join the rows. Press.

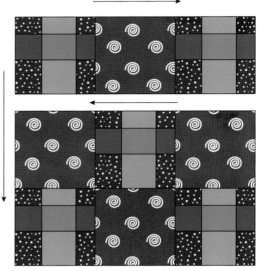

Quilt Assembly Diagram

2. Piece the 1" strips, using diagonal seams, to make 4 lengths, each approximately 36".

3. Starting at the left end of a 5" border strip, sew a narrow border strip to the lower edge. Press the seam allowances toward the 5" border strip. Repeat to make a total of 4 inner/outer border strips.

4. Attach the first border to the upper edge of the quilt as shown below. Leave approximately 8" of the strip unpinned to the quilt and allow the free end to extend beyond the right edge 5", plus a few inches.

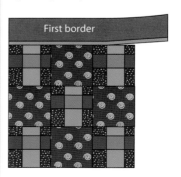

5. Stitch the partial seam. Press.

6. Add the second border to the left edge of the quilt, sewing all the way to the outer edge of the first border. Press. Repeat for the third and fourth borders.

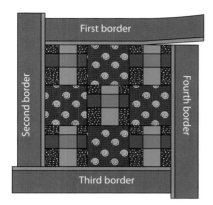

7. Return to the first border and finish stitching it to the quilt and to the fourth border. Press. Trim the excess length on each border to square up the quilt.

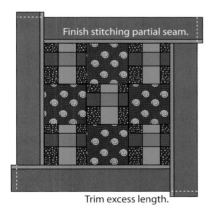

8. Layer the quilt top with batting and backing; baste. Quilt as desired. My quilt is channel quilted in the transparency blocks to accentuate the visual flow. The alternate blocks are quilted in a meandering pattern, and the border is stitched along every other black stripe.

9. Join the binding strips on the diagonal; trim the seam allowances and press open. Fold the binding strip in half lengthwise, wrong sides together, and press.

10. Attach the binding using your favorite method for making mitered corners and joining the ends. Whipstitch the binding to the back of the quilt. Label your quilt.

Lotus Leaves Squared

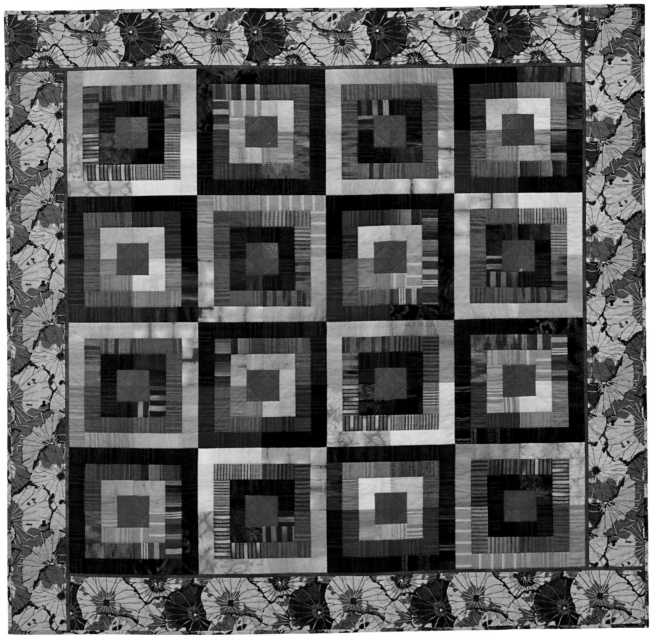

Designed and pieced by Christine E. Barnes, machine quilted by Carol Walsh, 2008.

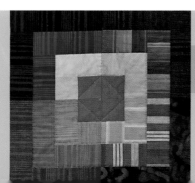

Finished block: 12″ × 12″
Finished quilt: 59¾″ × 59¾″

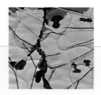

I can't think of a better quilt to make in the Color Club! You'll make sixteen basic blocks, then cut them through the center in both directions and reconfigure the units into seemingly complex blocks. Something magical happens when you slice your basic blocks and rearrange them, and sharing that experience with your quilting friends is a delight.

There's an easy-to-follow strategy at work here: Variations in value—light, medium, and dark—establish the design, while a variety of pattern styles and scales give the quilt a sophistication that belies its simple construction.

You'll need at least twelve each of light, medium, and dark values. Try for value consistency within each category—you want the lights to separate from the mediums, and the mediums from the darks. Working from my stash, I used a few additional fabrics in each value for more options. My quilt is made up of mostly stripes, batiks, and hand-dyes, but tone-on-tone or subtle prints in three distinct values can be just as effective.

Materials

Warm, intense, solid fabric: ¼ yard for the block centers

Light-value fabric: ¼ yard each of 12 or more fabrics for the blocks

Medium-value fabric: ¼ yard each of 12 or more fabrics for the blocks

Dark-value fabric: ¼ yard each of 12 or more fabrics for the blocks

Warm, intense, tone-on-tone fabric: ¼ yard for the narrow inner border

Naturalistic print: 1¾ yards for the outer border and binding

Backing fabric: 4⅛ yards

Batting: 68" × 68"

CUTTING INSTRUCTIONS

From the warm, intense solid:

Cut 16 squares 4" × 4" for the block centers.

From *each* light-, medium-, and dark-value fabric:

Cut 2 strips 2" × width of fabric.

From the warm, intense tone-on-tone:

Cut 6 strips ⅞" × width of fabric for the inner border.

From the naturalistic print:

Cut 4 *lengthwise* strips 5¾" wide and at least 57" long for the outer border.

Cut 5 strips 2½" × length of fabric for the binding.

Block Assembly

Press all seam allowances open when assembling the blocks, sewing the blocks into rows, and joining the rows. Pressing the seam allowances open allows you to join the units with greater flexibility, never worrying about which way the seam allowances go.

You will make two types of basic blocks, all built around a red center square. For 8 blocks you'll add light pieces to the center square for Round 1, medium pieces for Round 2, and dark pieces for Round 3. For the remaining blocks, you'll add the pieces in the reverse order: dark, medium, and light.

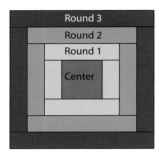
Basic block light/medium/dark

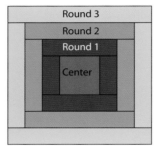
Basic block dark/medium/light

For *each* round, cut the pieces from the 2" strips of the *same* fabric.

Round 1: Cut 2 strips 4" long and 2 strips 7" long.

Round 2: Cut 2 strips 7" long and 2 strips 10" long.

Round 3: Cut 2 strips 10" long and 2 strips 13" long.

1. Start by making a light/medium/dark basic block. Sew 4" light pieces to the left and right edges of a center square. Repeat with 7" light pieces on the upper and lower edges of the unit to complete Round 1.

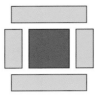
Round 1

2. Sew the 7" medium pieces to the left and right edges of the unit. Repeat with the 10" medium pieces on the upper and lower edges of the unit to complete Round 2.

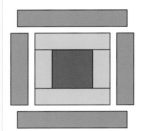
Round 2

3. Sew the 10" dark pieces to the left and right edges of the unit. Repeat with the 13" dark pieces on the upper and lower edges to complete Round 3. The block should measure 13". Repeat Steps 1–3 to make a total of 8 blocks with this value arrangement.

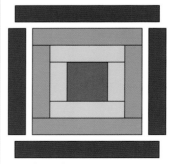
Round 3. Make 8.

4. Working in the opposite value order (center square surrounded by dark, medium, and light pieces), make 8 more blocks.

5. Carefully cut each basic block through the center in both directions to make 4 units, for a total of 64 units.

Cut.

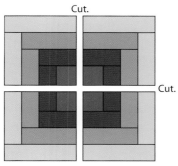

Cut.

Cut 8 dark/medium/light blocks to make 32 units.

Cut.

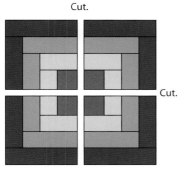

Cut.

Cut 8 light/medium/dark blocks to make 32 units.

 Tip

Your basic blocks will probably not measure exactly 13". To compensate, I carefully center a block on my rotary mat in (or over) an area 13" × 13", then cut it in half in both directions, using the lines on the mat as my guide. Cutting in this fashion, instead of working from the edge of the block, "splits" any piecing inaccuracies and makes it easier to join the units.

6. Working on your design wall, arrange the units so the light/medium/dark blocks alternate with the dark/medium/light blocks. I prefer to design the quilt unit by unit, rather than randomly making blocks and later trying to "make them work." With a unit-by-unit approach, you can best distribute the color and pattern across the surface.

7. Sew each group of 4 units together to make a block. Make 16 blocks, 8 of each value arrangement.

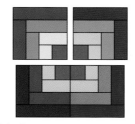

Make 8.

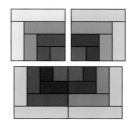

Make 8.

Quilt Construction

Refer to the quilt photo (page 52) and the Quilt Assembly Diagram below.

1. Sew the blocks into rows. Press. Join the rows. Press.

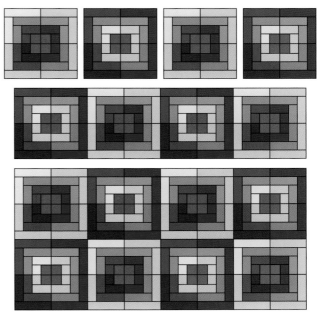

Quilt Assembly Diagram

2. Piece the ⅞" inner border strips using diagonal seams into 4 strips, each at least 57" long. Press the seam allowances open.

3. Sew an inner border strip to each outer border strip; press the seam allowances toward the outer border.

4. Attach the first inner/outer border to the upper edge of the quilt as shown below. Leave approximately 8" of the strip unpinned and allow the free end to extend beyond the left edge of the quilt 6", plus a few inches.

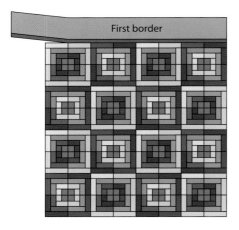

First border

5. Stitch the partial seam. Press.

6. Add the second border to the right edge, sewing all the way to the outer edge of the first border. Press. Repeat for the third and fourth borders.

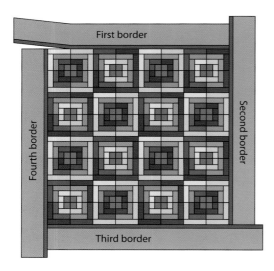

First border

Fourth border

Second border

Third border

7. Return to the first border and finish stitching it to the quilt and to the fourth border. Press. Trim the excess length on each border to square up the quilt.

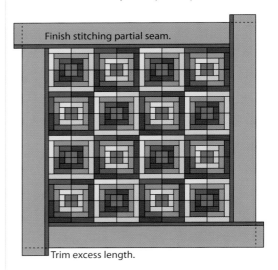

Finish stitching partial seam.

Trim excess length.

8. Layer the quilt with batting and backing; baste. Quilt as desired. My quilt is stitched in the ditch of the blocks and with a square on point in each red center. It's also stitched in the ditch on either side of the inner border, with meandering in the outer border.

9. Join the binding strips on the diagonal; trim the seam allowances and press open. Fold the binding strip in half lengthwise, wrong sides together, and press.

10. Attach the binding using your favorite method for making mitered corners and joining the ends. Whipstitch the binding to the back of the quilt. Label your quilt.

Luminaria

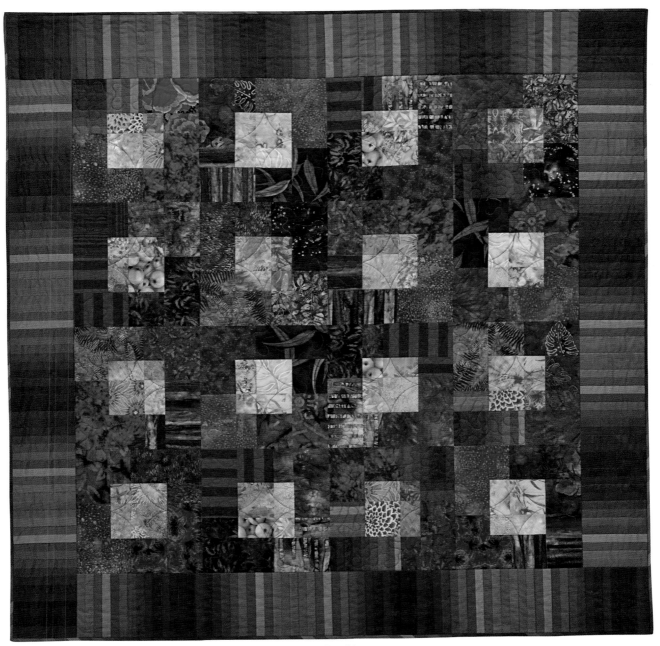

Designed and pieced by Christine E. Barnes, machine quilted by Carol Walsh, 2008.

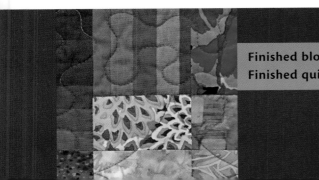

Finished block: 12½″ × 12½″
Finished quilt: 61½″ × 61½″

When it comes to the special effect of luminosity, color choices are everything: Warm, intense colors surrounded by cooler, duller colors just seem to glow (page 13). Certain fabrics with dappled color—in particular, batiks—help to create a luminous look. In this modular quilt you'll find lots of batiks, but I also used a few prints and stripes for variety and an element of surprise.

The materials list calls for sixteen fabrics in each of two broad categories—center and surround fabrics. I confess, however, that I used more than sixteen of each kind because a greater selection makes it easier to distribute the color and pattern across the quilt top.

I paired my center and surround fabrics with color harmony in mind. For example, a yellow-orange fabric with violet accents looks great surrounded by a violet fabric. To help you choose and pair your fabrics, review the color concepts of value, temperature, and intensity (pages 7–15).

Materials

Medium-value, warm, intense fabrics: ¼ yard *each* of 16 fabrics for the block centers

Darker-value, cooler, less-intense fabrics: ⅜ yard *each* of 16 fabrics for the block surrounds

Stripe: 1¼ yards for the border

Binding fabric: an additional ⅝ yard of border fabric for standard binding, or 1¼ yards for bias binding

Backing fabric: 4¼ yards

Batting: 70″ × 70″

 Color Cue

For your darker, cooler, less-intense fabrics, don't go *too* dark or *too* dull; a few brighter colors surrounding the warm colors will energize the design.

CUTTING INSTRUCTIONS

From each medium-value, warm, intense fabric:

Cut 1 square 4″ × 4″.

Cut 1 square 2½″ × 2½″.

Cut 2 rectangles 2½″ × 4″.

From each dark-value, cool, less-intense fabric:

Cut 2 strips 4″ × width of fabric.

From the border fabric:

Cut 6 strips 6″ × width of fabric.

From the binding fabric:

Cut 7 strips 2½″ × width of fabric.

Block Assembly

Press all seam allowances open when joining the pieces.

1. Begin with 4 warm, intense pieces cut from the same fabric and 2 dark, cool, less-intense strips cut from the same fabric. In the illustration on page 59, the warm, intense pieces are numbered; the cool, less-intense strip pieces are lettered. Cut the lettered pieces from the strips as you go, much as you would in constructing a Log Cabin block.

2. Sew Piece A to the upper edge of Piece 1. Trim the edges of Piece A even with the edges of Piece 1. Press. Add Piece B to the left edge of the unit. Trim. Press. Working counterclockwise, add the remaining strip pieces to the center pieces as follows:

Sew Pieces C and D to Piece 2.

Sew Pieces E and F to Piece 3.

Sew Pieces G and H to Piece 4.

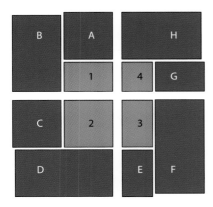

3. Repeat with the remaining pairings of center pieces and strips for a total of 16 sets of units (or more if you want additional units to work with).

Quilt Construction

Refer to the quilt photo (page 57) and to the Quilt Assembly Diagram at right. Press all seam allowances open when joining the units, blocks, and rows.

1. Now comes the hard part—and the fun! Working on your design wall, arrange the units all at once, striving to keep the same fabrics from touching. Use the Quilt Assembly Diagram at right as a guide, noting the orientation of the large squares.

 Tip

I like to lay out my quilt unit by unit, rather than sewing units into blocks and later trying to "make the blocks work." With a unit-by-unit approach, you can best distribute the color and pattern across the surface.

2. Once the units are arranged on your design wall, remove and sew each group of 4 units into a block. Press. Match the seams where the center pieces and strip pieces meet in each block, but don't worry about matching the seams at the block centers; slight inaccuracies won't be noticeable. Make 16 blocks.

Make 16.

3. Sew the blocks into rows. Press. Join the rows. Press.

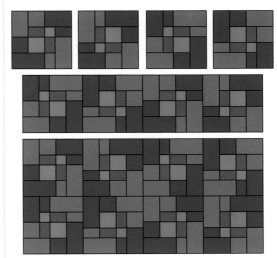

Quilt Assembly Diagram

4. Cut 2 of the border strips in half crosswise. Attach each half-strip to a full strip, matching the stripe pattern, to make 4 identical border strips, 6″ × approximately 60″.

5. To add the borders, see *Parfait Dreams*, Quilt Construction, Steps 2–5 (page 64).

6. Layer the quilt top with batting and backing; baste. Quilt as desired. My quilt is stitched in simple leaf designs in the warm center of each block, with meandering in the rest of the quilt.

7. Join the binding strips on the diagonal; trim the seam allowances and press open. Fold the binding strip in half lengthwise, wrong sides together, and press.

8. Attach the binding using your favorite method for making mitered corners and joining the ends. Whipstitch the binding to the back of the quilt. Label your quilt.

Parfait Dreams

Designed and pieced by Christine E. Barnes, machine quilted by Carol Walsh, 2006.

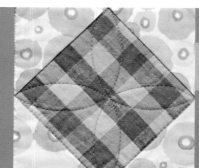

Finished main and alternate blocks: 7 1/16"
Finished quilt: 41½" × 41½"

The traditional Connecticut block, one of my favorites, inspired this scrappy quilt. Variations in value—lights, mediums, darks—make the pattern pop; warm and cool hues balance the visual temperature; bright and muted colors create a sense of depth.

The nine main blocks advance, thanks to the dark-value large triangles, all cut from fabrics hand-painted by Elin Noble. Lighter-value triangles surround the mostly medium-value, on-point center squares in these blocks. In the alternate blocks and setting pieces, softer colors shimmer.

There's even a touch of luminosity in three of the main blocks: The small triangles in the lower left, center, and upper right blocks glow, as if light is coming from beneath the surface. (See Luminosity, page 30, and Magic Fabrics, page 34.)

Materials

For 1 main block*:

Fabric A (medium value): 5″ × 5″ square

Fabric B (medium-light value): 4″ × 8″ rectangle

Fabric C (dark value): 7″ × 7″ square

*You will make a total of 9 main blocks.

For 1 alternate block and 2 side setting pieces**:

Fabric D (medium value): 4″ × 8″ rectangle

Fabric E (medium value): 4″ × 8″ rectangle

Fabric F (medium-light value): 8″ × 8″ square

Fabric G (light value): 8″ × 18″ rectangle

**You will make a total of 4 alternate blocks and 8 side setting pieces.

For 4 corner setting pieces:

Fabric D or Fabric E (medium value): 4″ × 8″ rectangle

Fabric F (medium-light value): 4″ × 8″ rectangle

Fabric G (light value): 8″ × 8″ square

Stripe: ⅞ yard for the border

Binding fabric: an additional ½ yard of border fabric for standard binding, or 1¼ yards for bias binding

Backing fabric: 3⅛ yards

Batting: 50″ × 50″

CUTTING INSTRUCTIONS

Main block

The directions that follow are for 1 main block. Repeat to make 9 main blocks.

From medium Fabric A:

Cut 1 center square, using the template (page 65).

From medium-light Fabric B:

Cut 2 squares, each 3⅜″ × 3⅜″. Cut each square once diagonally to make 4 half-square triangles.

From dark Fabric C:

Cut 1 square 6¼″ × 6¼″. Cut the square twice diagonally to make 4 quarter-square triangles.

Alternate block and side setting pieces

The directions that follow are for 1 alternate block and 2 matching side setting pieces. Repeat to make a total of 4 alternate blocks and 8 side setting pieces.

From medium fabrics D and E each:

Cut 2 squares, each 3⅜″ × 3⅜″. Cut each square once diagonally to make 4 half-square triangles of each fabric. (You'll use 2 of each in the alternate block and 2 of each in the side setting pieces.)

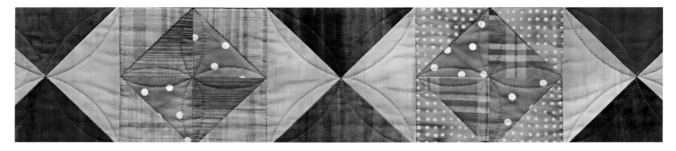

From medium-light Fabric F:

Cut 4 squares, each 3⅜″ × 3⅜″. Cut each square once diagonally to make 8 half-square triangles. (You'll use 4 in the alternate block and 4 in the side setting pieces.)

From light Fabric G:

Cut 2 squares, each 6¼″ × 6¼″. Cut each square twice diagonally to make 8 quarter-square triangles. (You'll use 4 in the alternate block and 2 in the side setting pieces, and you'll have 2 left over.)

Cut 2 squares, each 3⅜″ × 3⅜″. Cut each square once diagonally to make 4 half-square triangles. (You'll use all 4 in the side setting pieces.)

Corner setting pieces

The directions that follow are for 4 matching corner setting pieces.

From medium Fabric D *or* E (your choice):

Cut 2 squares, each 3⅜″ × 3⅜″. Cut each square once diagonally to make 4 half-square triangles.

From medium-light Fabric F:

Cut 2 squares, each 3⅜″ × 3⅜″. Cut each square once diagonally to make 4 half-square triangles.

From light Fabric G:

Cut 4 squares, each 3⅜″ × 3⅜″. Cut each square once diagonally to make 8 half-square triangles.

Border and binding

From the border fabric:

Cut 4 strips 6″ × width of fabric, for borders.

Cut 5 strips 2½″ × width of fabric, for standard binding.*

Note: For bias binding (shown on this quilt), cut a total of 4 strips 2½″ wide × longest possible bias.

Block and Setting Piece Assembly

MAIN BLOCK

1. To add the surrounding triangles (B) to the center square (A): Fold the center square, right sides together, in half both ways and crease the edges. Fold each triangle, wrong sides together, in half on the long edge and crease. (Handle this bias edge carefully.) Join opposite triangles to the center square, nesting the creases. Press toward the triangles. Add the remaining triangles in the same manner. Press.

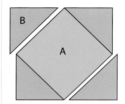

2. To add the large triangles (C) to the center unit: Fold and crease each large triangle as you did the smaller ones. Join opposite triangles to the center unit, aligning the crease in each triangle with the intersection of the small triangles. Press toward the large triangles. Add the remaining triangles in the same manner. Press.

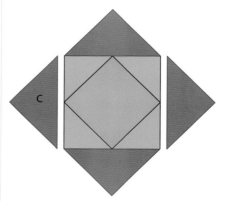

Main block

3. Repeat Steps 1 and 2 to make a total of 9 main blocks.

ALTERNATE BLOCK AND SIDE SETTING PIECES

1. Join a center triangle (D) or (E) and a surrounding triangle (F). Press. Make a total of 8 pieced squares, 4 of each combination.

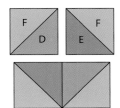

Make 4 of each.

2. Join 4 pieced squares, 2 of each combination, to make the center unit for the alternate block. (Set aside the other 4 pieced squares for the side setting pieces, Step 4.)

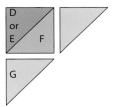

Make center unit.

3. Add the large triangles (G) to the center unit, creasing each large triangle as you did for the main blocks and centering the crease on the seam of the center unit. Press toward the large triangles.

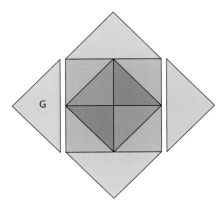

Make 1 alternate block.

4. Join 2 pieced squares, 1 of each combination, to make a rectangle unit. Press. Add 2 small triangles (G) to the sides of the unit. Press toward the triangles. Add a large triangle (G) to the remaining edge of the unit. Press toward the large triangle. Make 2 matching side setting pieces.

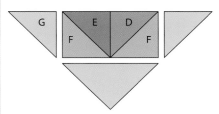

Make 2 matching side setting pieces.

5. Repeat Steps 1–4 to make a total of 4 alternate blocks and 8 side setting pieces.

CORNER SETTING PIECES

Join a triangle (D) or (E) and a triangle (F) to make a pieced square. Press. Add small setting triangles (G) to adjacent sides of the pieced square to make a corner setting piece. Press toward the triangles. Make a total of 4 matching corner setting pieces.

Make 4 matching corner setting pieces.

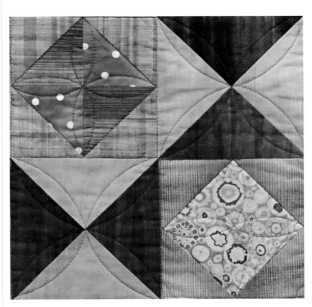

Quilt Construction

Refer to the quilt photo (page 60) and to the Quilt Assembly Diagram below. Alternate pressing directions in adjacent rows.

1. Join the blocks and side setting pieces into diagonal rows. Press alternate rows in opposite directions. Join the rows. Press. Add the corner setting pieces. Press toward the corners.

Quilt Assembly Diagram

2. Attach the first border to the upper edge of the quilt as shown below, centering the stripe pattern (see project photo on page 60). Leave approximately 8″ of the strip unpinned and allow the free end to extend beyond the left edge of the quilt 6″, plus a few inches.

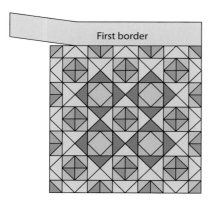

First border

3. Stitch the partial seam. Press.

4. Add the second border to the right edge, sewing all the way to the outer edge of the first border. Press. Repeat for the third and fourth borders.

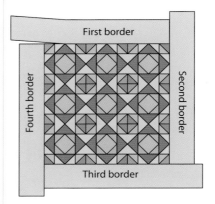

First border

Fourth border

Second border

Third border

5. Return to the first border and finish stitching it to the quilt and to the fourth border. Trim the excess length on each border to square up the quilt.

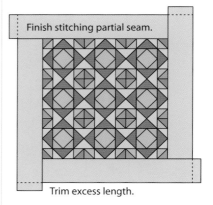

Finish stitching partial seam.

Trim excess length.

6. Layer the quilt top with batting and backing; baste. Quilt as desired. My quilt is stitched in the ditch, with a curvilinear pattern in each main and alternate block. The border is stitched along every other stripe.

7. Join the binding strips on the diagonal; trim the seam allowances and press open. Fold the binding strip in half lengthwise, wrong sides together, and press.

8. Attach the binding using your favorite method for making mitered corners and joining the ends. Whipstitch the binding to the back of the quilt. Label your quilt.

Parfait Dreams template; includes seam allowance

Woven-Color Vest

Designed and made by Christine E. Barnes, 2010.

Raw-edge strips weave in and out to make the fabric for this blended-color vest. Narrow stitching along the edges of the warp (lengthwise) and weft (crosswise) strips, followed by vertical channel stitching, secures the strips and prevents raveling. Flat yarn, which resembles narrow ribbon, finishes the lengthwise raw edges.

It's easiest to weave both left and right vest fronts at one time, as mirror images, with their center front edges facing. You'll work the strips over a foundation of osnaburg, an inexpensive, roughly woven needlework fabric available at full-service fabric stores; be sure it's all cotton. Osnaburg usually comes in a natural color.

I used my Kimono Collage Vest pattern (available on my website, christinebarnes.com) for this project, but you can use any lined vest pattern without darts, with or without a collar.

The fabrics in my vest blend just enough to be harmonious, yet not so much that they look like one piece. Be willing to cut a few practice strips and weave them—you can't predict the effect until you work the fabrics together. You'll be surprised.

Materials

Vest pattern of your choice

Main fabric: 2 × the length of the vest pattern front, from the highest point on the shoulder to the lower edge, plus ¼ yard, for front warp strips and vest back

All-cotton osnaburg: same yardage as main fabric, for the foundation*

Stripe: ½ yard for weft strips

Tone-on-tone fabric: ½ yard for weft strips

Soft plaid: ½ yard for weft strips

Black-and-white print: yardage specified on your pattern, for collar and ties, typically ¼ to ½ yard

¼" flat rayon yarn: enough to couch the warp strips on each front; this vest required 4½ yards.

Thread: to blend with flat yarn

Lining fabric: yardage specified on your vest pattern

Rotary cutting equipment: ruler, cutter, and 24" × 36" or larger mat, helpful for weaving the strips

Masking tape

Basting glue

Walking foot (not required but very helpful)

Fabric marker that shows on your main fabric

*Preshrink twice, to remove sizing and to give the fabric a softer hand and more tooth.

CUTTING INSTRUCTIONS

From the main fabric: Cut and set aside enough fabric for the vest back, plus 2" extra in length to allow for shortening of the fabric during channel stitching. Use the remainder of the fabric for the vest fronts. Do not cut out the fronts at this point. Leave the fabric whole with the vertical fold line in it.

From the osnaburg: Cut pieces equal in length to the main fabric front and back pieces.

From the stripe: Cut as many weft strips as needed for your vest fronts (one strip is enough to weave across both front pieces at once). My vest has 3 striped weft strips for the fronts, but your vest may require more. Cut the lower weft strip 4″ wide to allow extra fabric for a seam allowance at the bottom of the vest. Cut the other weft strips 3″ wide.

From each of the tone-on-tone and soft plaid: Cut as many 2½″ weft strips as needed for your vest. My vest has 3 weft strips of each fabric.

Cutting the Main Fabric into Warp Strips

Rather than dealing with separate warp strips on the vest fronts, you'll cut them to within 2″ of the lower edge of your main fabric. Keeping the strips attached at the bottom makes it easier to weave accurately. I use the lines on my rotary mat to draw straight, accurate lines on the fabric.

1. Lay the main fabric right side up on your rotary mat and secure the upper and lower edges with tape. Draw a horizontal line approximately 2″ from the fabric's lower edge and perpendicular to the center fold line.

2. Mark a vertical line 1″ to the left of the center fold and 1″ to the right of the center fold, stopping exactly at the lower horizontal line. This 2″ buffer-zone strip will make your weaving easier. Next, mark a vertical line 4″ on either side of the buffer strip, again stopping at the horizontal line. Mark as many more lines, each 3″ apart, as needed for each vest front. (You'll have leftover fabric on each side.) Remove the tape at the upper edge and carefully cut along the vertical lines to the horizontal line with scissors. Remove the fabric, which will now resemble a fabric hula skirt.

Main fabric warp strips

3. Press the osnaburg foundation fabric lightly to smooth it but not so much that you flatten the texture. Place it on the mat and secure the upper and lower edges with tape. Place your "skirt" on top and pin it to the foundation at the lower edge. Arrange the strips so they are straight, with raw edges touching.

4. Fold the buffer strip down to expose the foundation; repeat with *every other* warp strip. Lay the 4″ weft strip on top of the remaining warp strips and the foundation, aligning the lower raw edge of the strip with the horizontal line.

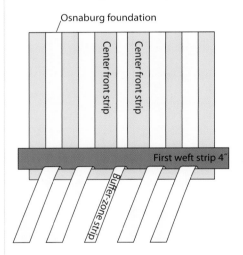

5. Bring the warp strips back up to cover the weft strip and the foundation; check the alignment of all strips and straighten the weft strip at the horizontal line, if necessary.

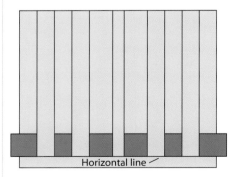

6. Fold *down* the warp strips that were *up* in Step 4, and lay a 2½″ weft strip on top of the other warp strips and the foundation. Bring the warp strips back up to cover the weft strip and foundation; check the alignment of all strips and straighten, if necessary. Repeat the process with the other 2½″ weft strip. Repeat the sequence of weft strips until you reach the top.

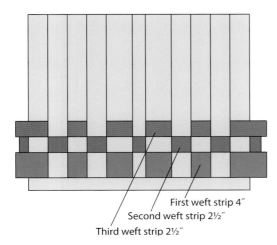

First weft strip 4″
Second weft strip 2½″
Third weft strip 2½″

7. Look at your weaving and correct any wavy strips, "snugging" them where they intersect. Use dots of basting glue under the raw edges to tack the warp and weft strips to each other. Pin to secure all layers—foundation, warp, and weft.

8. Using your walking foot, stitch close (⅟₁₆″) to all raw edges, in both directions. (If you don't have a walking foot, you'll need to pin more.) Between the vertical stitching, channel stitch equidistant lines. Your walking foot may be just the right width to use as a guide.

9. Use dots of basting glue to tack the rayon yarn over the raw edges of the warp strips. Using a medium-length, medium-width zigzag stitch and thread to blend, couch the rayon yarn.

10. Cut the fabric for the vest back wide enough to accommodate the back pattern piece, plus several inches. Layer the fabric and foundation; pin. Channel stitch the back as you did the fronts.

11. Cut out *one* vest front, placing the *seamlines* of the pattern piece so the center front warp strip and the lower weft strip will be 3″ wide when the seams are sewn. *Turn the pattern piece over* and cut out the opposite, mirrow-image vest front. (If you have ever accidentally cut two right vest fronts, you know the heartbreak of that mistake!)

12. Cut out the vest back.

13. Construct the vest according to your pattern directions.

FRAME IT!

A great way to showcase your color work is to take mock blocks you make in the Color Club and turn them into fused or sewn blocks and then frame them.

You may wonder if putting fabric under glass is an issue. I don't worry about it because I change my framed pieces as I create new blocks or collages with new fabrics. A faint film occasionally accumulates on the underside of the glass, but I wash the glass before reusing it.

My blocks are stitched to a foundation of muslin or graph paper, but not quilted. (On smaller blocks, I leave the graph paper in place for stability.) Alternatively, you can fuse your fabrics to a muslin foundation. I create my collages on card stock or other substantial paper, then cut out and mount the collage on illustration board.

Here are the components you'll need to frame your work:

Frame. Metal framing pieces are sold by pairs and in 1-inch increments.

Mat. For my blocks I selected white. If you desire a white mat and your fabrics contain white or cream, match the mat to the white or cream in the fabrics. If you decide to use a colored mat, select one that harmonizes with a main color in your block.

For a square block, cut the mat so all sides are equal in width. On a rectangular composition, allow an extra ½˝ at the bottom if possible.

Glass. I use standard nonglare glass. Museum- and conservation-grade glass cut down on ultraviolet light more but are typically double the price.

Mounting board. For a collage like Kimono Collage, (page 71), you'll need illustration board. With a block or group of blocks, the foam-core backing (see below) can double as the mounting board.

Foamcore backing. Choose ⅛˝ thickness if you're using a separate mounting board; otherwise, go with ³⁄₁₆˝ thickness.

Hardware. The hardware and assembly instructions come with the framing components; hangers and wire are sold separately. Choose the wire gauge based on the weight of your finished framed piece.

Assembly

1. Inspect the block or collage to make sure it's free of thread; press.

2. Center the block or collage on the mounting board or foam-core backing and check the placement by laying the mat on top; lightly tack the block or collage to the board or backing with a dab of glue at each corner.

3. Carefully place the mat on top, followed by the glass, making sure the frosted side of the glass is facing out. If you've mounted your piece on a separate board, add the foam-core backing underneath. Set aside this "sandwich."

4. Follow the instructions included with the frame components to join the top piece to the sides; leave the lower piece off. Turn the frame face-down on your work surface.

5. Carefully pick up the sandwich and turn it over. Working from the open end of the frame, slide all layers into the tracks until everything is snug and in place.

6. Slide the lower frame piece into place, making sure all layers of the sandwich are caught in the frame track. Tighten the corner screws and attach the hanging hardware.

Concentric Squares, 16″ × 16″, designed and made by Christine E. Barnes, 2010.

Watery batiks for the "rounds" and a woven plaid for the center square have a dreamy effect. Framing a block composed of squares accentuates the design. This block was sewn to a muslin foundation.

Kimono Collage, 16″ × 24″, designed and made by Christine E. Barnes, 2005.

A fabric "sketch" for a full-size vest takes on a life of its own as a framed collage. The raw-edge fabric pieces are composed on a paper pattern, then lightly fused rather than stitched.

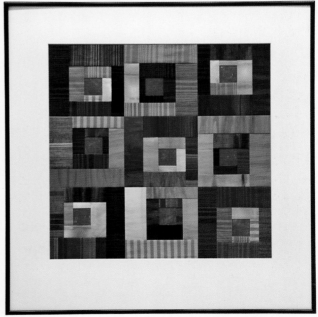

Off-Beat Nine Patch, 25″ × 26″, designed and made by Christine E. Barnes, 2006.

Designing and making these paper-pieced 6-inch blocks was so much fun that I went on to make *Squares and Stripes*, page 36.

Who doesn't love going to a quilt show—on your own or with quilting friends? Think of this chapter as a Color Club field trip, the culmination of your exploration and experimentation with color.

Sea of Sofas, 63" × 68", machine pieced, appliquéd, and quilted by Sandra Poteet, 2009.

Upholstery scraps combine in this fanciful underwater composition, inspired by the curved-piecing technique of German quilt designer Dorle Stern-Straeter. The lighter-value, high-contrast border recedes, thanks in part to seaweed and octopus shapes that spill onto the "frame."

Chromatosis III, 50″ × 39″, created and machine quilted by Linda Waddle, 2006.

This wholecloth quilt displays an exquisite array of closely related values, warm colors, and naturalistic motifs. Linda hand-dyed the fabric, then screen-printed, stenciled, and stamped her designs to create depth and movement. Rayon and polyclear threadwork gives it sheen and texture.

Cactus, 47" × 18", painted, appliquéd, and machine quilted by Velda Newman, 2003.

Subtle variations in value, temperature, and intensity lend sophistication to the organic forms in this art piece. Knots formed from waxed-cotton cording accentuate the texture of the hand-painted cotton duck.

Photo by Jay Daniel

Bellagio Pumpkins, 28½" × 21½", fused, machine appliquéd, and machine quilted by Sarah Sherwin Roberts, 2009.

Light, medium, and dark values give definition to the forms in this curvilinear composition. An analogous scheme of red, red-orange, and orange is both warm and intense; true and new-neutral (page 21) grays and black provide context and visual relief.

Spines & Thorns, 47″ × 47″, fused, pieced, and machine quilted by Barbara Chernos Edelson, 2005.

When it comes to color, this quilt has it all: A cool, light-value background recedes, making the high-contrast blocks appear suspended in midair; a sliver of warm, intense color delineates each block. A few of the abstract "fronds" intrude upon the blocks, adding to the illusion of depth.

The Cubist's Edge, 36″ × 48″, machine pieced and quilted by Frances Holliday Alford, 2009.

Violets, greens, oranges, pinks, and blue-greens play off each other in a palette of near-triadic (page 25) hues. Frances began her design with twelve individual blocks, then cut them randomly and reconfigured the units to capture the essence of the colors and forms. Satin stitching, machine felting, overlays, and photo transfers embellish the surface.

Sassafras Spirits, 52″ × 52″, pieced and machine quilted by Elaine Plogman, 2006.

The deeply lobed leaves and small bluish fruit of the Sassafras tree sparked Elaine's vibrant palette of warm and cool hues. The large-scale rectangles were sun-printed using actual leaves and fabric paint; other fabrics were air brushed. Elaine makes use of the advancing and receding aspects of color in her design: The pieced blue border recedes, while intense blocks framed by dark-value strips advance.

Cellular Structure VI, 40″ × 81¼″, fused, pieced, and machine quilted by Sue Benner, 2007.

High-intensity colors, warm and cool, pulsate in the presence of black and other dark-value hues. Intriguing textures and patterns accentuate the positive and negative space. Sue dyed and painted silk, cotton, and found fabrics to create the large-scale forms.

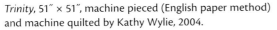

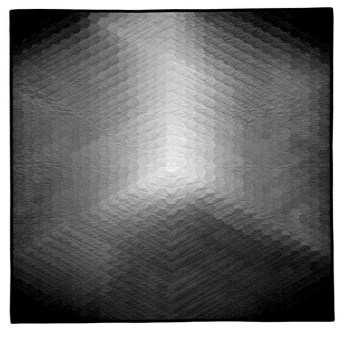

Trinity, 51″ × 51″, machine pieced (English paper method) and machine quilted by Kathy Wylie, 2004.

A computer, inkjet printer, and pretreated fabric sheets were the tools Kathy used to tell the story of color in this stunning quilt. The edges of the center hexagon radiate into six "paths" of color, three for the primaries and three for the secondaries, with every possible combination in between. Value plays a role, too: From white at the center, the hues gradate to black at the edges.

Poppies on the Bluff, 45″ × 33″, pieced, machine appliquéd, and machine quilted by Coni Hendry, 2009.

A stand of poppies and seedpods overlooking the Pacific Ocean "just said quilt" to Coni. Medium- and dark-value background fabrics intensify the pink poppies and yellow-green pods. A free-and-easy mix of patterns befits the casual, soft-edge appliqué technique.

Unopened, 40″ × 32½″, fused, machine appliquéd, and machine quilted by Roxane Lessa, 2009.

Hand-dyed fabrics by the artist and a few commercial fabrics portray an angel's-trumpet flower just before blooming. Warm hues range from yellow through red-violet; cool sky and foliage fabrics balance the visual temperature. Fabric paint and threadwork bring out highlights and suggest shadows.

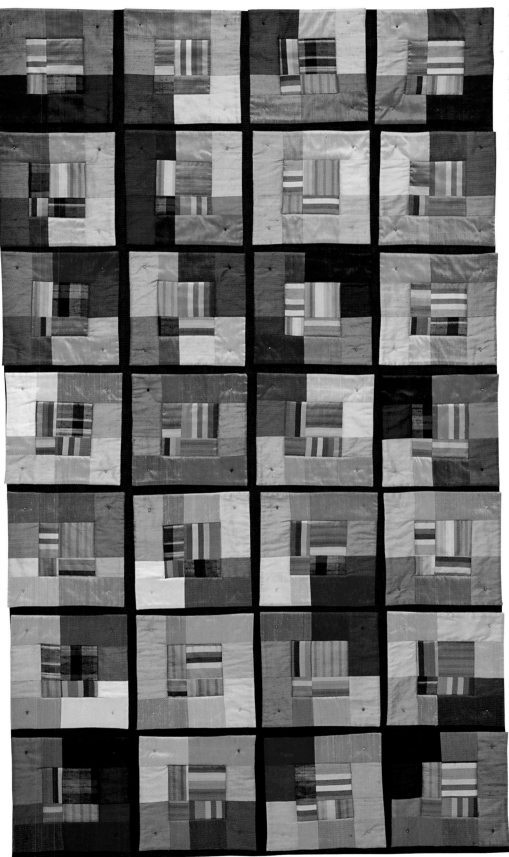

Facets, 44″ × 77″, pieced and machine quilted by Karin Hannickel, 2003.

Like the polished planes of cut gems, these dimensional silk tiles dance in the light. The individual "quilts" are lined and anchored to the foundation with stitching at each center square and glass beads at the corners.

Ripples in the Water, 39½″ × 30″, pieced and machine quilted by Joyce Doo Teekell, 2007.

A triad (page 25) of blue-violet, yellow-green, and red-orange is enhanced by a handful of other hues in this jazzy composition. A solid black background and black-and-white patterns pull it all together. Joyce used techniques she learned in a workshop taught by Carol Taylor.

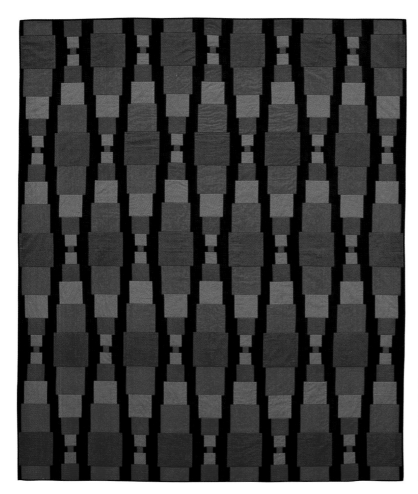

Black Widow, 67″ × 82¾″, pieced and machine quilted by Patrice Sims, 2008.

Intense versions of orange, red-orange, red, and red-violet form an analogous color combination (page 22) in this bright, bold quilt. Black, a true neutral, tempers the strong colors and establishes the design. The fabrics were hand-dyed by Patrice.

Luminosity Expanded, 55″ × 55″, pieced, machine appliquéd, and machine quilted by Ardis J. Tobin, 2010.

Narrow black-and-white sashing bisects the blocks in Ardy's adaptation of *Luminaria* (page 57). For her unique take on the pattern, Ardy grouped units of similar hues to form cohesive squares of radiant color. A low-key pieced border plays a supporting role.

Ma Belle France, 38″ × 40″, pieced, machine appliquéd, and machine quilted by Diane Ansel, 2005.

Diane's landscape captures the vibrant color and casual charm of the south of France. Intense blues in the sky, hillside, and sea balance the red-oranges, oranges, and yellow-oranges typical of French village architecture. Diane began her quilt in a workshop by Velda Newman.

Old Pecos Cabin, 48½" × 35", fused, appliquéd, and machine quilted by Michelle Jackson, 2009.

Red-violet, violet, and blue-violet highlights give this architectural landscape its rich glow and sense of mystery. Michelle typically works from a photo she has taken but often adds one or more colors that aren't naturally present. In the photo that inspired this quilt, the violet areas were a washed-out gray. Note how the binding changes to match each edge for an expansive, uninterrupted image.

Doors of Rome, 24½" × 33½", Kim Butterworth, 2007.

Warm, earthy hues mingle with cool blue-grays in Kim's urban landscape. Photos from a trip to Italy were printed on cotton, then constructed as fiber tiles, a technique Kim adapted from Julie Hirota. Tiny copper beads attach the tiles to a background collage that includes scripted upholstery fabric, a commercial fabric printed in a weathered-brick pattern, and organza.

Santa Barbara Riviera, 36" × 48", appliquéd and machine quilted by Ranell Hansen, 2009.

This landscape quilt breaks with conventional wisdom, which suggests using lighter values for distant elements. Here, darker-value gold and violet hills frame the city scene and imply late-afternoon light. Ranell was inspired by the work of painter Richard Schloss.

Expanding Star, 79″ × 77″, pieced and machine quilted by Judy Mathieson, 2006.

A nontraditional approach to value placement—lighter-value rays against duller, darker-value background fabrics—makes this stunning star quilt glow. A few cool rays among the many warm ones balance the temperature; black adds visual weight to the inner star. An Art Deco gate served as the spark for Judy's design.

Filigree, 95″ × 95″, paper pieced and machine quilted by Marilyn Badger, 2009, from the *Thistle Pods* pattern by Judy Niemeyer Quilting Inc.

A simple color combination dazzles when pieced in dupioni silks and batiks. Marilyn's intricate quilting with metallic threads forms a lacy overlay that frosts—but never overpowers—the design. Slight variations in the light-value background batiks add to the ethereal effect.

Mixed Messages, 41" × 41", paper pieced and hand-quilted by Jan Soules, 2009.

Diverse pattern styles and scales mix it up in this original blade design; a handful of scripted fabrics deliver the "message." The somewhat random use of color and value from block to block establishes a casual, carefree mood. Extending the outer-block fabrics beyond the inner border to the edges of the quilt has an expansive effect.

Aspen Solace #1 and #2, 78" × 40", pieced, fused, and machine quilted by Patty Hawkins, 2008.

Strong contrasts in value and texture establish the foreground and background in Patty's glowing diptych quilt. An array of materials and techniques—hand- and shibori-dyed cottons, deconstructed screen printing on cotton, screen-printed silk organza, and black tulle over each quilt—depict the interplay of light and shadow among the aspens of Colorado.

Earthscape, 28" × 36", fused by Christine E. Barnes, machine quilted by Carol Walsh, 2007.

Value, temperature, and intensity (pages 7-15) all play a role in this abstract collage. Light-value fabrics hand-painted by Elin Noble read as sky; dark-value foreground fabrics depict the volcanic landscape of Kilauea; an orange sun suggests a sulfurous atmosphere. Inspired by the mixed media art of David Barnes.

Sunrise Serenade, 41˝ × 43˝, machine appliquéd and quilted by Barbara Barrick McKie, 2006.

Barbara's exquisite depiction of a dahlia with morning dew displays a subtle blend of soft complementary color: yellow-green and red-violet, yellow-orange and blue-violet, red-orange and blue-green. The cotton sateen shibori background was hand-dyed by Barbara; the bloom, created using the disperse dyeing process, began with a digital photo she took in her garden.

Stars, 94" × 93", pieced by Sue Hengl, machine quilted by Elaine Beatty, 2007.

Sue's quilt, based on the traditional Martha Washington Star block, proves that all colors go together when you have lots of them. Contrasts in pattern scale (small, medium, and large) and style (traditional and contemporary) help to differentiate the pieces within each block. The majority of the stars were pieced by Sue; some were acquired in a block swap among members of her mini-group, the Poolside Quilters.

96 Hearts, 68" × 68", pieced and appliquéd by Nancy Miller, machine quilted by Bonnie Hunter, 2009.

Primary yellow, red, and blue look even fresher with the addition of secondary green, a "bridging color" (page 18). Made from Sandy Klop's American Jane pattern *Bee Mine Quilt*.

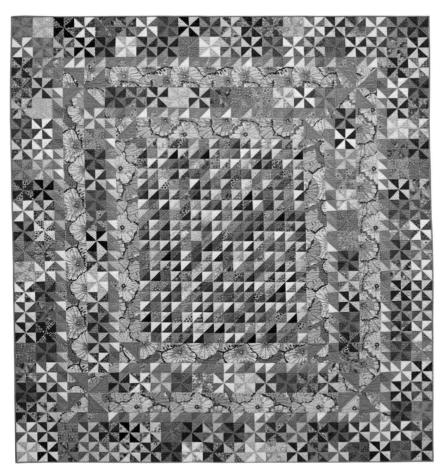

Fonthill Quilt, 76" × 84", pieced and machine quilted by Kerstin Stauffer, 2009.

Cool blues, blue-greens, and greens are balanced by complementary pinks (a light-value red), corals (a light-value red-orange), and other warm hues. The large-scale lotus leaf pattern spaces out the small-scale blocks for visual relief. Kerstin made her quilt using the pattern of the same name in Kaffe Fassett's book *Passionate Patchwork*.

Unselfconscious Stars, 84" × 86", pieced and machine quilted by Lynn Cooper, 2008.

A liking for the unexpected in traditional patterns led Lynn to yellow, gold, and pink for this sparkling star quilt. The intense background fabric and lighter, airier sashing also go against conventional choices, adding to the sense of fun. Lynn's design expands on a pattern by Catherine Kypta.

Log Pile Shadows, 42½" × 29", pieced, machine appliquéd, and machine quilted by Louisa Robertson, 2006.

There's another kind of transparency (pages 32-33), one that doesn't involve parents or children. This slice quilt looks as though sheer strips of color lie over sections of the image. The quilt was based on a photo and constructed by Louisa and her minigroup.

Wings: A Benefit Quilt for Humbolt Wildlife Care Center, 70" × 70", machine pieced, appliquéd, and quilted by Jody H. Rusconi, 2009.

Jody's 25 years as a jewelry designer and appraiser show in a palette that hints at sapphire, garnet, tourmaline, and quartz. Strong contrasts in value establish the pattern, which was inspired by the work of Karen Stone.

Crossover Color: Blue Stripe Vest, designed and made by Christine E. Barnes, 2005.

Twin-needle stitching along the stripe pattern gives this asymmetrical vest actual texture. For the collar, strips of indigo Japanese cotton link sections of colorful hand-dyed and patterned fabrics. The vest was made using Vogue pattern 8000.

Paper-pieced blocks decorate the back of the vest and the sides, below the square-cut arm openings. A cotton lamé stripe connects the blocks and makes a smooth visual transition to the body of the vest.

Birds of a Feather, pieced, machine appliquéd, and machine quilted by Marylee Drake, 2009.

The hand-dyed fabric serving as the foundation for Marylee's vest reminded her of the late-afternoon sun in the forest. Birds depicted in brighter yellow-green, blue-green, and red-orange reiterate the background colors in a bolder way. The vest was made using Judy Mullen's pattern More Than a Vest.

Felted Circles, designed and made by Christine E. Barnes, 2009.

Low intensity unites hand-dyed fabrics in lots of different colors; a more intense yellow-green foundation sets off the muted hues. The soft circles were created by teasing apart lengths of novelty wool yarn into roving, then needle felting them with a machine attachment.

FREQUENTLY ASKED COLOR QUESTIONS

The Color Club is the perfect setting for brainstorming color problems and finding solutions. Following are questions that come up frequently as quilters work (and sometimes struggle) with color. As you might expect, basic color concepts—value, temperature, intensity—and the color wheel often hold the answers.

Will a great mock block make a great quilt?

Not necessarily. If your mock block is intense or highly patterned, an entire quilt composed of identical blocks may overwhelm. Consider spacing out your pieced blocks with plain or simpler alternate blocks, in lighter values or less-intense colors. (See *Tile Dance*, page 40.) Then your "diva" blocks will float on a receding backdrop, creating depth and providing welcome visual relief, as in *Inside Looking Out* (page 9).

How can I achieve color variety?

Are you tempted to make yet another green and orange quilt? Look to the color wheel and the color combinations for a fresh approach. To green and orange, for example, add violet to turn the combination into a triad of secondary colors (page 25). To magenta (red-violet) and olive (yellow-green), add accents of deep iris (blue-violet) and mango (yellow-orange) for a double split complement (page 24). The color wheel is a terrific tool for quilters. Use it!

What is a *color recipe*?

I first came up with this term when trying to merge the concept of a repeat-block quilt, where all the blocks are the same, with my love of scrappy quilts. Here's how you might use a value recipe: In a quilt composed of star blocks, make all of the center squares medium in value, the star points dark, and the backgrounds light, but use different fabrics, in different colors, from block to block.

You can also maintain consistent values *and* colors: In a star quilt, make all of the center squares medium red, the star points dark green, and the background light "wheat" (pale yellow), but use different fabrics from block to block. With either plan, your quilt will feel both cohesive and spontaneous.

It's one of my favorite fabrics, and it's gone!

Unless you need a certain fabric for specific pieces in your quilt—in which case you'll need to beg your friends, visit every quilt shop within driving distance, or scour the Internet—this is not a problem. Trust me: Wonderful fabrics are out there just waiting to be your next favorites. And chances are, adding a new fabric to your quilt plan will make it even better.

Why does my quilt look flat?

Value is probably at the root of the problem. Most quilters have an abundance of medium-value fabrics; that's what fabric manufacturers produce because that's what we buy. Plus, fabrics that look distinctly different on the bolt quickly blend when cut up and sewn. Strive for more contrast in value, more lights and more darks, to give your quilt depth.

Contrast in other elements enhances the sense of depth and dimension. Warm colors (page 12) tend to advance and cool colors recede; intense colors (page 14) seem close, while low-intensity colors feel distant.

My quilts are all predictable. How do I get out of this rut?

Mix it up with different kinds of fabrics. I love combining batiks with stripes or hand-dyes with commercial fabrics. Different fabrics convey color differently, and diversity takes a quilt far beyond a focal fabric and its companions. The latter approach has a well-deserved place in quiltmaking, such as when you want to make a quilt for a room with an existing color scheme or a theme quilt for your nephew. But an element of surprise adds life to any quilt.

What can I do for the border?

For borders on my quilts, I usually use a fabric that doesn't appear elsewhere—it sets off the blocks and allows them to breathe. I also suggest a slightly lighter-value, less-intense fabric for the border. Why? Light-value, low-intensity colors recede, making the quilt feel open and airy. Just don't go too light or too dull, or the borders will look wimpy. Audition, audition, audition border candidates to find that just-right fabric.

Also consider adding "spinning borders" like the ones in *Parfait Dreams* (page 60) and *Squares and Stripes* (page 36). Having one end of each border strip extend to the edge gives a quilt a sense of motion.

I've tried everything, and my quilts are still boring.

You can take several steps to develop your sense of color. First, study the quilts that appeal to you—in this book, at quilt shows, at your guild's show-and-tell—and look for color cues in each one. My other advice is simply to use a greater number of fabrics, a move that will automatically bring unexpected dashes of color, pattern, and texture into the mix and enliven your quilt.

Finally, just keep trying. A background fabric that's a little lighter in value sets off your blocks and makes them dance; a warm, bright fabric sparkles amid cooler, duller ones; a geometric print tames a large-scale floral. On your own or in a group, work with your fabrics until you find the magical mix—you may be only one fabric away from a fabulous quilt.

Christine's first sewing memory, at age six, was asking her mother if she could make doll clothes out of the kitchen curtains. A few years later, she was dunking scraps of fabric into beet juice to get just the right pink (which, of course, didn't last). Her young interests matured and eventually led to degrees in costume design and journalism, followed by a career in writing decorating, soft furnishings, and remodeling books for Sunset Publishing. Between book projects, she followed her real passion, color and quilts. Christine's work has appeared in *Threads, American Quilter, Quilters' Newsletter,* and *Fabrications,* a British quilting magazine. Her first book on color, *Color: The Quilter's Guide,* was published in 1997. She has been lecturing on color and teaching color workshops for quilters since then.

Other pursuits revolve around her home, which has been featured in several Sunset books, including *Reinvent Your Kitchen, Color for Your Home,* and *Faux and Decorative Painting.* Her latest interest is framing contemporary modular pieces and collages.

Christine lives in Grass Valley, California, with Jeffrey and Bernard, her cat and dog. You can reach her at christinebarnes.com.

Great Titles *from* C&T PUBLISHING

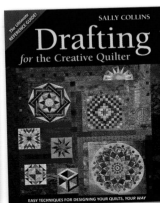
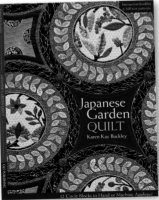
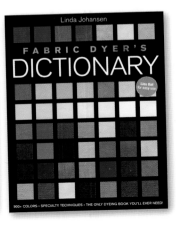

Available at your local retailer or **www.ctpub.com** *or* **800-284-1114**

For a list of other fine books from C&T Publishing, visit our website to view our catalog online.

C&T PUBLISHING, INC.

P.O. Box 1456
Lafayette, CA 94549
800-284-1114

Email: ctinfo@ctpub.com
Website: www.ctpub.com

C&T Publishing's professional photography services are now available to the public. Visit us at www.ctmediaservices.com.

Tips and Techniques can be found at www.ctpub.com > Consumer Resources > Quiltmaking Basics: Tips & Techniques for Quiltmaking & More

For quilting supplies:

COTTON PATCH

1025 Brown Ave.
Lafayette, CA 94549
Store: 925-284-1177
Mail order: 925-283-7883

Email: CottonPa@aol.com
Website: www.quiltusa.com

Note: Fabrics used in the quilts shown may not be currently available, as fabric manufacturers keep most fabrics in print for only a short time.